FOREST SCHOOL AND
ENCOURAGING POSITIVE BEHAVIOUR

of related interest

Forest School and Autism
A Practical Guide
Michael James
ISBN 978 1 78592 291 6
eISBN 978 1 78450 595 0

**How to Get Kids Offline, Outdoors,
and Connecting with Nature**
200+ Creative Activities to Encourage Self-Esteem,
Mindfulness, and Wellbeing
Bonnie Thomas
ISBN 978 1 84905 968 8
eISBN 978 0 85700 853 4

**Teaching Social Skills Through Sketch Comedy
and Improv Games**
A Social Theatre™ Approach for Kids and Teens
including those with ASD, ADHD, and Anxiety
Shawn Amador
ISBN 978 1 78592 800 0
eISBN 978 1 78450 820 3

**Positive Behaviour Management
in Primary Schools**
An Essential Guide
Liz Williams
ISBN 978 1 78592 361 6
eISBN 978 1 78450 704 6

FOREST SCHOOL AND ENCOURAGING POSITIVE BEHAVIOUR

Outdoor Education Skills for Pupils
with Additional or Complex Needs

David Rylance

Jessica Kingsley Publishers
London and Philadelphia

First published in Great Britain in 2022 by Jessica Kingsley Publishers
An imprint of Hodder & Stoughton Ltd
An Hachette Company

1

Copyright © David Rylance 2022

A CIP catalogue record for this title is available from the British Library and the Library of Congress

ISBN 978 1 83997 078 8
eISBN 978 1 83997 079 5

Printed and bound in Great Britain by CPI Group

Jessica Kingsley Publishers' policy is to use papers that are natural, renewable and recyclable products and made from wood grown in sustainable forests. The logging and manufacturing processes are expected to conform to the environmental regulations of the country of origin.

Jessica Kingsley Publishers
Carmelite House
50 Victoria Embankment
London EC4Y 0DZ

www.jkp.com

CONTENTS

Chapter 1

INTRODUCTION TO THIS BOOK

It is my hope that you have in your hands a book that will be useful to you in a number of ways. Perhaps most importantly the tips, suggestions and philosophy contained within will mean that you can run a forest school provision where children can benefit from what you (and nature) have to offer, regardless of any additional needs they have. But also, for those of you who are just starting out in forest school, this book will provide a solid foundation from which you can build your provision. What I fervently hope too is that you can find the skills to make your work enjoyable. Working with young people whose behaviour is challenging is tough. I know many teachers and teaching assistants who can find the stress overwhelming. It can chip away at your resilience over time. But the truth is we can all learn how to manage difficult and challenging behaviour with skill and flair, and reduce the stress we feel as a result. That is my chief role when I work as a behaviour consultant with schools and other provisions – to move colleagues from 'I don't know what to do next' to a better place.

Forest school is a (relatively) new element to the education approach in the UK and, indeed, wider world. Managing challenging behaviour, however, seems to be an age-old issue! You may be reading this book as a forest school leader who works in a school, perhaps as a teacher or teaching assistant. For you, I can confidently say that you will find much within these pages that will be of value in your forest school provision and other outdoor lessons, but that you will also gain a useful perspective and many strategies and techniques that will be of use to you in the classroom too, with a little adaptation at most.

If you are reading this book as an operator of a privately owned forest school provision, offering a service to schools, youth groups and other organizations, you too will find much to assist you in this role. Many of your customers will appreciate a forest school provider who can cater to special educational needs and disability (SEND) and complex needs. The skills contained within these pages will mean you can be assured of an effective approach to support these learners. For your 'mainstream' attendees, you will see how presenting yourself in a certain way can mean you manage poor behaviour by never having any to deal with! And of course, your skills will be appreciated by parents and they'll bring their children back; in my opinion (and parents tell us this), Out There Adventures, where I work, benefits from this. There are many good-quality providers out there, but I also believe that it is often other skills that will make parents come back for more.

If you are a newly qualified forest school leader, then you will already be aware of the ethos around behaviour that is part of the forest school way. You are at the perfect stage of your forest school career to build on and consolidate your skills by reading this book! If you can use even a small number of the skills and techniques within, making them your own, I can tell you that you will be streets ahead of many, many educators and forest school leaders, in my experience. What a great way to start! And remember that when you create an ethos in your forest school that will support the more complex children, then you will also find that you will be supporting all learners to make the best behaviour choices they can.

All forest school leaders should (must) be reflective practition-ers, constantly aware and curious, always testing their approaches, always looking for new ones. We all need a high level of awareness, all day. Is there a learning opportunity to grasp? Why is that child doing that? How should I approach this? How can I...? You get the picture! So, read on, enjoy the book, reflect on the ideas and skills within and be ready to use them out there in the woods to benefit those children who need, perhaps more than most, what you will have to offer.

About a week before I wrote this part of the book, I was standing in the woods while a nine-year-old threw logs at me, one of which hit me in the head, another in the ribs. His driving issues, I felt, stemmed from a lack of resilience and an obsession with control. My analysis of the situation was that he had realized I was not going to make choices driven by him, and was looking to escalate the situation. I explained to him, in a calm and neutral tone, that I would withdraw my attention from him until he was ready to re-engage. My attention mattered to him only because I was retaining control of it; otherwise, I am fairly sure he couldn't have cared less.

In my head was a single worry – that he might force my hand, perhaps by trying to leave the woods, pushing me to intervene, or per-haps try to really hurt himself (he had already been hitting his head against things). I hoped we wouldn't get to that, as I was desperate not to reinforce the message that if adults couldn't be controlled, he could 'up the ante' and then they would cave in. My understanding from talking to his carer was that this was something he had experi-enced before, and so a negative behaviour choice had been embedded and become habitual, as it had been successful in the past. The boy had grown to like the heady experience of being in charge, even when he was surrounded by adults. Key for me was the mantra that we can have total control over a huge part of an interaction with others, that part being the behaviour choices we make.

In truth, I remotely monitored him in my peripheral vision, while effecting disinterest, taking pictures of plants, becoming en-grossed in bark patterns on old trees, tidying the forest school site (it was already tidy, but you get the picture...). He watched me closely, and on occasion when he thought I was watching would try to catch my attention with rather dramatic behaviours.

After about ten minutes of this he wandered across to where I was and asked me what I was doing. Carefully monitoring the pace, pitch, tone and volume of my voice, I cautiously explained I was getting ready to carry the equipment back out of the woods. We'd already had this situation; he had started the session well, assaulted me, re-engaged, and then thrown firewood at me. I didn't want a repeat of this. As I pulled the trolley along the track, I nodded to one bag of equipment left on the woodland floor. 'I can't carry that one.' Without waiting for a response, I walked away; he picked up the bag and followed along. When his carer arrived, I was pushing the cart, the child was in the cart with the equipment, and we'd had a short discussion about what had happened and were now laughing together. He was keen to return to the woods in the future, to attend his 'one-man forest school'.

I mention this for a number of reasons. I wanted you to see that I certainly don't get it all my own way, and probably never will. Working with such complex children has been my job for over quarter of a century. Sometimes it goes really well. Other times it doesn't. Sometimes all the planning in the world can only make so much difference. And I have unshakeable faith that, given time, I can help this child to be successful and to manage behaviour choices in a more effective and positive way, and the woods will be part of that process.

Chapter 2

A BRIEF INTRODUCTION TO FOREST SCHOOL

I sometimes have to be careful when I'm explaining my preferred approach to forest school with a headteacher who is holding the purse strings (tightly)! The reason? I like to run my days according to the true principles of forest school whenever I can, where children lead the learning. But I'm cautious about saying I like to do it with 'lots of resources and tools, but no plan'! Of course, in the main I'm pushing against an open door and a lot of school leaders know the value of education beyond the delivered curriculum. But we do live in an outcome-driven world and education is not exempt from this. I certainly do get school leaders saying, 'Yeah, but what certificate will they get out of this?' Thankfully this is rare, and we do offer outdoor learning other than 'just' forest school in these situations.

The reason for this approach is straightforward: at its most simple, forest school is a child-centred and often child-led approach to learning, and by learning I mean that in its widest sense. Experiences, connections, instincts, senses, all play their part. Forest school, then, should be a long-term, regular activity, where children can explore, increase their confidence, take measured risks, improve their self-esteem and become more resilient. All of this happens in the natural environment, and while this does not need actually to be a forest, trees are part of that environment. There is, of course, lots of evidence of the benefits of woodland on our health and wellbeing, and I don't intend to dwell on this now. Suffice to say that the outdoors, and woods and forests in particular, has a positive impact on us.

Forest school happens regardless of weather conditions, with perhaps the obvious exception of strong winds (we usually then use woodland margins, beach school or sheltered wild places). The learners then experience their woodland in sun, rain and snow. They should also experience seasonal changes. The environment is frequently the catalyst for learning, inspiring children and young people to explore flora and fauna, material properties and hands-on experiences. We can see, then, that much traditional outdoor learning can be included in forest school, but also that there is more to forest school than that. Children may go pond-dipping as part of their science curriculum, or as part of forest school, but a typical science field trip is not designed to address the wider, holistic education of the child in the way that forest school is. And a pond-dipping hour is not always forest school, although it might happen during a forest school day.

Forest school is not about pouring knowledge into a learner's head from a pre-set list of 'things they should know'. It supports, instead, that holistic learning: social, emotional, spiritual, physical and intellectual development are all nurtured. At its core for me, often, is a remarkable improvement in resilience in children and a strengthened self-belief that comes from managing risks, of many kinds, and simply 'being' in the natural world. Learners will overcome challenges of many kinds and at many levels, appropriate to them. This is important; no two children will experience the same forest school day. Self-reflection will ensure this, of course, and we as forest leaders should encourage it. For example, for some children a rainy autumn day can be a huge challenge to their resilience; for others, it is just an experience to absorb, and for yet others, it's a delight. The most effective forest school leader is not there to supply instant solutions, but rather to support children to find solutions of their own and then ultimately to see these children apply their recently developed skills to new experiences and situations. After all, we cannot predict the future with any confidence; we can only really guarantee uncertainty in the future. Perhaps it makes sense to prepare our learners by equipping them with lively, curious and confident minds that will enable them to face and overcome the challenges inherent in this uncertainty.

Play is an important element of forest school but, of course, this means different things to different people, children included. We keep this in mind as forest school leaders, or else we run the risk of applying our own perspective on play to the experiences of others. Some children might be peripheral to group play, and that is exactly where they want to be or are comfortable being. Forest school allows for this. We don't put pressure on them at this point (certainly not in most cases – there might be exceptions and we will discuss them later). Of course, some adults might view complex learners as a risk during free play, to themselves or others, and we should be careful with such assumptions; in forest school we look at risks and benefits, mitigate where necessary and take it from there. Some teachers might feel the same about letting 'certain' learners lead their own learning! In fact, as we will discuss, these children might need such opportunities more than others...

So how might a 'typical' forest day look? (Easy answer: there's no such thing.) Well, perhaps a group of children have donned their coats and wellies and trooped out of class, chatting about what they want to do. Maybe they've found a wren's nest in some brambles. The forest school leader hears this chat and asks a few 'I wonder' questions. 'I wonder how you start a bird's nest?' 'How do you secure the first few twigs in place?' 'What makes a good spot for a nest?' And that's it; the range of possibilities for some of the children has come down to this – let's give it a try. Of course, some learners have other ideas. Some seem to 'just' play, yet others drop in and out of all the different activities that are going on. There's collaboration, problem solving, assessment and negotiation going on. Sensory feedback is high; this material is too stiff, this bark is raspy. Some children look for quiet places, getting engrossed in an activity – that 'soft fascination' that learners sometimes exhibit, when their interest is on one thing, to the exclusion of all else.

During all of this, the forest school leader is on hand as a guide, facilitator and supporter. Maybe just before lunch, the leader will ask the right questions of the children, in a review of the morning. This will focus on the practical, social, emotional and other elements of what has gone on, and might serve as an impetus for the continuing efforts in the afternoon, or even a complete direction change if that's where the learners lead us! Further review opportunities will present later in the day, at group or individual level, and the astute leader takes them all. The leader will also have some ideas on standby for those children who want them, and will have a lively, curious and enquiring mind of their own, such that new ideas will pop into their heads based on observations of the natural environment around them, which they can choose to share with the learners. These might stimulate a different direction to the day's events, or not. The very best of leaders will know how to adapt activities and suggestions to support more complex learners to be able to access opportunities that might otherwise be denied them, and make behaviour choices that also do not prevent them from making the most of their learning.

Some teachers I know would be horrified at the thought of such a day! But of course, structure is there if you have the eyes to see it. Risk is measured alongside benefit, and managed with awareness. Crucially, learning is truly happening – no 'jolly in the woods' is this...

I can understand, of course, that the prospect of such a powerfully learner-led approach might seem daunting, especially if you are working with SEND learners or children with complex issues. Equally, SEND practitioners know that there are desirable outcomes we want for these children and while pouncing on opportunities as they occur is something such specialists get very good at doing, I do feel there are times when our forest school leader role requires us to be more direct in how we manufacture or manipulate learning and development opportunities. In fact, I would argue that we owe it to our SEND learners to work in this way; many of them have had previously missed learning opportunities, many are at a disadvantage or playing catch-up relative to their peers. While I'm entirely happy with the idea (in forest school and in learning generally) that children learning at their own pace is the best way, I also want to expose them to experiences that can accelerate their holistic learning when I can. I have a range of ideas for activities that can do that, some borrowed from more 'traditional' outdoor learning experiences, some from the world of bushcraft and so on. For example, children learn about fire at forest school. They understand how to be respectful of it, how to harness its qualities, perhaps for campfire cooking, boiling water for a cuppa or keeping warm. I'll offer them opportunities to have a go at fire lighting for themselves, perhaps using a ferrocerium rod and striker with cotton pads, which will require effort, focus, persistence, resilience and a continuing development of these traits. I might suggest a team effort: the Group Bow Drill Challenge (more on this later) that requires trust, communication, resilience (again), review and analysis skills (I use the plan-perform-evaluate model) and more. All learners can and do benefit from this, but I know such an activity will be a precious opportunity for SEND children and those with complex issues. So, while forest school has some core principles, and some observers would say, if they aren't in place, then what you're doing 'isn't forest school', I would argue that the semantics matter much, much less than the results. In my experience, this can become even more important with older children too, who perhaps have deeply embedded habits of making poor behaviour choices. We shouldn't miss opportunities for these young people through worrying about the 'purity' of the forest school principles inherent in what we are doing. I must admit to being saddened at times when I see leaders seeking advice, perhaps in social media groups, only to be told 'that's not forest school'. Be very careful, if you are such a purist, that your approach does not deny access for some learners. Remember also, that the leader who asked the question just needs an answer, and not to be preached at...

Forest school is therefore that outdoor space, complete with a fire area, wild places to explore, natural materials and opportunities that allow learners to develop a deep connection with the natural world. In forest school, they can explore with all their senses the sounds, textures and other qualities of their environment and develop the skills that will prepare them for the world and its uncertainties. For SEND children, we can use forest school to help us to close the gaps in their learning, not in terms of curriculum content but in supporting them to develop the traits they need to face the curriculum without fear. We can do this in ways which the classroom almost inevitably cannot. Read on; we will now explore how that can be done.

Chapter 3

FOREST SCHOOL: SUPPORTING BEHAVIOUR CHANGE

In this chapter, we will explore how the outdoor woodland environment can and does benefit a broad range of children and young people, including those with SEND or complex needs. But we will also see that all children benefit from being out in nature, including those who have no diagnosis but can display challenging behaviour. Often, these are the children that Richard Louv, author of the wonderful book, *Last Child in the Woods*, would say are suffering from 'nature deficit disorder'.[1]

I have personally had some quite astonishing experiences of the effect of nature on children. To recall just a few, I was supporting a colleague running a forest school session with kindergarten children, and the head of that kindergarten was there with a video camera, recording a particular child. She informed me that the child had selective mutism and she wanted to record this for parents as it was their first day in the woods. This was at approximately 9.45am. By 11am, this same child was lying on my back, arms around my neck as we crouched over some small, electric blue feathers (it was a bird

---

1   Louv, R. (2010). *Last Child in the Woods*. London: Atlantic Books.

of prey kill site, which I didn't mention at that time). He was asking me question after question: what did the bird look like; how big was it; could we find more feathers? The bird, a jay that had undoubtedly come to a sticky end, had nonetheless contributed wonderfully to the experience this boy had on that day, enough to bring a lump to my throat and tears to the eyes of the kindergarten head as she recorded this. It was an amazing moment. Even more amazing is the fact that I have seen many very quiet, withdrawn, non-communicative children respond to the woods in this way, enough for it not to be a coincidence. I've also worked with inner-city teens who found their time whittling spoons round the campfire to be the most precious part of their week. They could leave behind the image, bravado and attitude, and just be in nature. It is a privilege to be involved in such things, and I know many forest leaders who have had similar experiences.

There is no doubt that being 'in nature' can have a hugely positive impact on humans. There is an abundance of research around this and I encourage you to seek some of it out, but I am sure that anyone reading this book will not necessarily need to. You will all know the value of nature because your own experiences will resonate with the evidence out there. You will have experienced the calm mind that goes with the simple act of sitting against a tree in the woods, letting your mind empty and just being. One of the activities I like to do with all ages, from nursery age children up to adults, is to ask them to find themselves a 'sit spot' in the wood. Usually I recommend they are outward facing, so that they limit distractions from others, but it's often not needed. Once people have experienced this, they can use the spot whenever they need it, and will, over the weeks, choose to go to their sit spot. Children will do this spontaneously (I always ask them to, as a minimum, let me know they are doing this!), and older children and young people sometimes ask to have the opportunity built into each day, such is their liking for it. I have noted that many children will use their sit spot when there has been an issue of some kind, either during the forest school or even before they arrive. It becomes a safe, contemplative place. You as a leader can even advise a child to use it in this way. I'd suggest this should not be as a consequence of poor behaviour, of course. I do know leaders who have such a spot; a place where children can go to consider their behaviour, reset their emotions and then return to the mix. While I don't usually do this, I have on occasion, and I've seen it used skilfully by many; you can't argue with success. But it's not the woodland equivalent of 'the naughty step'! Also, it isn't a punishment, like sitting outside the headteacher's office, so do not be tempted to use it as such. Do that and you risk undermining the intrinsic rewards of being outside, and that would be unforgiveable.

So let's consider further how forest school can help children and young people who regularly display challenging behaviour.

On arrival at forest school for the first time, children find themselves, in most cases, in an environment that is not their usual one, if not downright alien to them. This can result in a range of responses, of course, including heightened anxiety, over-excited behaviour, caution and, for some, a little fear. It's our job, obviously, to manage this and most forest school leaders do this through gentle introductions to the woodland. There are basic techniques to do this which you may recall from training: activities such as 'one, two, three where are you?' that introduce boundaries, for example.

The new environment offers us further opportunities rather than just setting boundaries beyond which learners do not wander. Most children will be attentive to you as the leader and guide at this time, especially if the surroundings are unfamiliar. Using this time to begin to embed routines and expectations makes a lot of sense, as we need to pounce when they are attentive, particularly those who have an attention deficit!

The environment is a great leveller. All of the children will have a similar starting point. We will have seen the anxiety that can come with playing catch-up with peers; this is far less of an issue when all of the learners have yet to learn anything! I used to notice this a lot teaching traditional outdoor activities such as canoeing or surfing to first-timers. Everyone will get it wrong; everyone makes mistakes and that is alright. If we are clever, we ensure that attitude never changes in forest school.

Think of this time as a 'fresh start' for all of the young people in attendance. Maybe they already know you and maybe they don't; it really doesn't matter that much. Make sure they all understand that they have a 'clean slate'. You will base everything you do on what you see from this point on, and past history is not relevant. So the level of trust you can have in them, the level of responsibility that might be given, and the subsequent activities they might get to do, will all be based on the behaviour choices they make from this point on. Remember, many children who display challenging behaviour can come to you with a reputation, and many of them know this. Giving this clean slate can be a huge relief for them and I have even used it with young people who have found themselves in the criminal justice system. All of them proved, when attending forest school, that they could be very different people from their usual persona, the face they present to the rest of the world.

I've spoken to a number of leaders beyond the colleagues I usually work with and there are some common behaviours that they see, not necessarily with regularity but more often than others. These are often simple things like walking off with tools (and for this you just need to develop and embed the routines that don't allow for this like putting knives in holders, closing saws before moving anywhere, having consistent places to put tools collectively, doing tool counts). Squabbles, particularly with younger children, seem also to be an issue. In this case, a great leader I know, Richard Wood, initially uses the 'keep 'em busy' approach; they don't have time to get into squabbles! Over the time they work with him, children know something exciting will happen when they get to the woods, and it is this anticipation which engages them, not disagreements with peers. He constantly monitors behaviour, wonders why it is happening and acts according to his conclusions. This dictates his manner; as he says, 'My direction is like a river; could be wide and slow; could be full on and fast.' That's a great way to think about how you are a performer as a forest leader. As a result, behaviour issues are few, and of course when they happen, there's a plan. Rich uses the Thoughts-Feelings-Actions model to talk through this, and the I ASSIST model for intervention: **I**solate (the children from their audience and each other, if appropriate); **A**ctively listen (pay attention to what the drivers for the behaviour might be, rather than what you think they are); **S**peak calmly and assertively; use **S**tatements of understanding (to show you've made no judgements); **I**nvite the young person to consider the impact of behaviour choices, possible alternative choices they could have made; then give **S**pace and **T**ime, to reduce pressure. It's a great model I'm sure many leaders use, but it's worth repeating here! It's a way to manage incidents successfully, build emotional intelligence over time and reduce problems in the long term. It reminds us that an unfortunate incident can still give us an opportunity to find a positive, and this is often that we have grasped it as a learning opportunity.

Chapter 4

MANAGING YOUR OWN BEHAVIOUR

Okay, so this chapter could fit in any book about behaviour management regardless of whether you're a forest school practitioner, a parent, a classroom teacher, a police officer, or whatever. This is true because managing behaviour, at its core, is about human interaction. We need to recognize that as part of our perspective before we proceed much further. Then we need to consider that we have 100 per cent control over 50 per cent of that interaction: us! This is a real positive when you think about it; we are already in a good position to influence the outcome of a situation for a positive result. Simply put, we should always manage that element of an interaction over which we have the most control; that is, ourselves. In fact, as I mentioned earlier, we need to lay to rest any suggestion or belief that we have control over the behaviour of others. Remember, we can influence the choices children make, we can make it easy for them to make good choices, and even hard for them to make poor ones, but ultimately we can only really control ourselves. Also of course, our employer expects us to be able to manage ourselves (and rightly so), as professionals, and would take a dim view of our inability to recognize the need for us as the adults to be the ones who can stay calm.

I should also stress at this point that I am not suggesting that when behaviour is less than perfect at your forest school, this means it is your fault. That would be unfair, and sometimes the most meticulously planned sessions can go wrong, or even be sabotaged, especially when complex needs are incorporated into your group. The caveat I would add, though, is that any reflective practitioner (teacher or forest school leader) will know that there are times when they could have made different choices that could have resulted in different outcomes. Of course, we've all got it wrong from time to time and we should never give ourselves too much grief about it, as that's how we learn. We just need to ensure we don't endlessly repeat the same mistakes – that would turn a wonderful job into one you dread!

Modelling our expectations to the group is really very important; it sends the message that we really care about behaviour at our forest school. I once watched an adult shouting at a girl of about 11 years old, 'I don't care how angry you get, you don't shout at people!' Hardly a great example of practising what you preach! Needless to say, we had a conversation later... We cannot tell children that they can achieve their goals through being calm, respectful and patient, and then try to achieve ours through other means. That just won't work. Not because it might not be effective in the short term; it certainly might. But because it will send the message that what you are asking of the children is not what you truly believe, it's just for show. It is important to remember that when we respond to unwanted behaviour, our perspective will colour our attitude. This will drive our own behaviour in response, which in turn elicits an attitude and subsequent behaviour response from the child. This can lead to damage to the relationship, conflict and problems. But it can also, if our perspective is good, lead to improved relationships, mutual respect and better behaviour choices. That is why the section 'A structure to your behaviour approach' in the next chapter is so important. The child who deliberately runs in the fire circle could be seen as determined to provoke you, or as someone who is anxious about the environment and keen to be removed! Perspective matters; it would be poor practice to manage those two situations in the same way.

Most of you will know this old story, which has many, many forms, but I think it is ideal to illustrate a point here, and my version goes something like this:

A Native American grandfather is sitting talking to his grandson. His grandson has been telling him that he struggles sometimes with his temper and asks his grandfather's advice. The old man tells him, 'There are two wolves living in your heart. One is caring, thoughtful and considerate; the other is malevolent, spiteful and unpleasant. These two wolves are constantly battling for control over you and your decisions.'

'Which will win, grandfather?' the boy asks.

'Whichever one you choose to feed the most', says his grandfather.

We must realize that we always have a choice with our behaviour, as professionals and as people. Be under no illusions that in your role as a forest school leader, you will not come across children who will 'push your buttons'. In my observations of schools across the age range, forest school practitioners and others working with young people, I see evidence suggestive of this regularly. I've definitely been guilty of allowing this to happen to myself, so make no judgements! Negative displays of behaviour, especially towards the extreme end of the range of possibilities, can often result in this. But, as we've seen, perspective is key and we can train ourselves to get this right. It may take a while; there may be lapses where we inwardly kick ourselves, but remember that every time we get it wrong, just like children, that's another opportunity to learn and to strive to get it right next time! While aiming, of course, to reduce the number of times we get it wrong...

In this goal, our challenging learners are our greatest resource. After a long day in the woods, my colleagues and I will reflect on events. We've known each other long enough and respect each other enough to be fairly blunt with each other without damaging the relationship. We can see when a situation, group or individual has got under the skin of a colleague. We will always look for solutions that have improved relationships as a desired outcome. It's not about Leader A not being placed with Group B because there are issues. It's about seeing the value in striving for a positive future where A and B work together productively. As a team, we know that it is more effective to view these difficulties with that lively and positive curiosity that says, 'Wow, that caught me off guard! How can I make this better?' When we are successful with that tough situation, we are building the foundations for our approach with the next challenging group, and that means less time needs to be spent in establishing a healthy working balance, and more can be spent on great experiences. Everybody wins, and that is a great outcome.

When you come across that child or group then – the one that just seems to get under your skin, and bring out the other side to your usually positive and happy self – take the time to remind yourself that you can make things better. Indeed, it is very empowering to know that you will make decisions with your behaviour that will mean you ensure a positive experience for all. Be determined to find a way through a situation; be determined that the child who doesn't seem to like you is actually going to have you written indelibly into the top of their list of favourite adults in the future. Relentless positivity, high expectations and belief are key components of this approach. Last week was tough; today is a fresh start. Standards are set high because you know they are capable of achieving this, and you believe you can support them to make the better choices needed.

Chapter 5

DEVELOPING YOUR BEHAVIOUR TOOLBOX FOR FOREST SCHOOL

We have already recognized that, as a forest school leader, you might already be an employee of a single school, or a contracted provider to many. Whatever your circumstances, you will know the importance of the behaviour element of your forest school if you think back to the emphasis it was given during your training. This is not accidental; one of the benefits of forest school that we have already discussed lies in the inherent value the outdoors can have in reducing stress and anxiety, which are both drivers of behaviour choices everyone makes. But we also need to consider carefully what we want behaviour to look like in our forest school, and this might need to be entirely different from how your classroom is run. The reason for this is that when we step outdoors, we alter several factors that impact on behaviour in terms of context, and the possible functions of behaviour choices. For example, although there is evidence that green spaces reduce anxiety, some children, especially those who live in an inner-city environment (and a surprising number of older children), can find that, at least initially, anxiety can be heightened. If we accept that most of us make poorer behaviour choices when in a state of anxiety, then clearly we need to take account of this potential in our forest school. A child who begins to display belligerent, confrontational behaviour needs consideration. Is this belligerence only happening on forest school days; is the function of their behaviour to achieve the desired result of them being told to return to class?

For teachers who are struggling with complex young people in class, perhaps learners with SEND, running forest school presents an opportunity to change this. If what you are doing in class is not working, do you intend to carry on doing it in the outdoors? Or do you see this new venture as an opportunity to bring about change?

As an external provider (and it doesn't matter too much whether you are using the school grounds, or the children are coming to your venue), you would be wise to consider your behaviour toolbox because, while it is easy to agree that the management of behaviour remains with the accompanying school staff, in practice this is a struggle. Some classroom staff, in my experience, will also see it as a time to relax a little; I've even had a teacher bring marking with them during forest school! If you are providing your services to several schools, you can find yourself trying to operate in a number of different ways, but this won't work with all schools. It is far better to develop your own approach, and share this with the school, and naturally with the learners. I should say, of course, that this does not mean you do not make yourself aware of the school's behaviour policy. Ensure that you ask for an up-to-date copy of this document from a client school rather than relying on the version they (should) have on their website being the one they currently use...

So for all these reasons, we need to prepare a workable behaviour strategy – 'winging it' will not pass muster. Let's look at underlying principles before we start to examine practical strategies for the toolbox.

A structure to your behaviour approach

Notwithstanding what we've already discussed, first, it is important that you are aware of the behaviour protocols that are the norm (hence the need to see the behaviour policy), if you are providing forest school to a school or nursery group. If you are employed there as a teacher or teaching assistant, then the leadership might expect you to stick to those expectations. If you are coming in as an external provider, it is still good practice to familiarize yourself with the norms, even if this is just a brief chat with staff prior to the first session. I say this because I have worked with primary schools that have a 'no touch' policy, which can make some tasks difficult in forest school, including coaching with tool use. I have also worked with schools where shouting is the norm! For me, shouting at children is counterproductive and, except in cases of emergency, I do not allow it in my forest school. So, it's best to know of any behaviour protocols like this in advance.

My approach, whatever the norms of the provision (school, youth group, home-educated group), is this: I will explain how I approach behaviour, and that I will 'set my stall out' with the group, so that they are not confused when and if my approach differs from the one that they are used to.

With regard to an underlying theme, when it comes to behaviour, I use the same approach here as I do in class, or if I'm working with children from a school discussing behaviour, or if I'm delivering living history lessons dressed as a Roman legionary (all of which can happen in a typical working week for me)! My approach, underlying the practical toolbox, is this:

- I prefer to be proactive, rather than reactive.

- I maintain a high level of awareness at all times. I'm never off duty until the last child has left the site and another adult has taken responsibility for them and their behaviour.

- I keep everything firm, fair, friendly and positive.

This approach to behaviour in outdoor learning underpins the whole book, but let's start by looking at the advantages of being proactive.

Being proactive is our ultimate target. In my early career, I would get the opportunity to observe the behaviour ninjas in our school (a name which I later adopted for a classroom management app I created). These were the staff who never seemed to struggle with behaviour. I naively thought that if I used my free periods to observe these ninjas, I'd see lots of useful strategies I could try. Instead, I saw young people who, climbing the walls in other rooms, would calmly do their work, speak respectfully to staff and their peers and enjoy the lessons. What I eventually realized, thanks to patient mentoring from these colleagues, was that they had already done all of the hard work, pre-empted problems, put interventions in place, reduced triggers for poor behaviour choices, set their room out in the most effective way, adjusted their teaching style, and taken lots of other small but significant pre-emptive measures.

I spoke recently to a friend and superb forest school leader about this book, and talking of the approach and perspective that underpins our toolbox, he told me, 'With certain groups, I'll know they might lack attention, so I'll take them on a route to the fire area that minimizes distractions, or I might embrace a distraction as part of the journey into the wood.' Both approaches are pre-empting the problem. If we agree that 'People in glass houses shouldn't throw stones', then perhaps it's equally fair to say, 'People who are likely to throw stones shouldn't get put in a glass house'! We work hard not to set our children up to fail, by thinking ahead.

So, while saying that the best way to deal with behaviour problems is not to have them in the first place might sound a little smug, it is a fine target to aim for. Of course, we will have strategies for the 'What do I do when...?' moments, but, ultimately, we aim to minimize the need to use them. How do we do this? Read on, and also read the chapters on practical techniques for SEND that follow!

At this point, I'd also like to share with you a set of mantras that were taught to me pretty early in my teaching career. Back then, I'd just left the military and possessed a very black and white, 'head down and charge' sort of mentality, which I quickly found was worse than useless with the young people I worked with, who were all excluded from mainstream schools, volatile and had no 'respect for authority' in the traditional sense. Then I attended some training by a gentleman named Rob Long who shared these three mantras with us:

· Analyse, don't personalize.

· Fight fire with water.

· The problem is the problem, not the child.

These were like an epiphany! They resonated deeply. In every instance where I'd got it wrong (there were many...), or seen others get it wrong, I could use the mantras to discover why. When I'd occasionally (mostly accidentally) got it right, or seen other colleagues do so, these mantras were at the heart of the solutions. Since then I've shared these mantras with thousands of professionals and parents and never found fault with them, or situations where they were not relevant. So I share them with you as forest school leaders knowing they will be useful to you, and invite you to explore them in a little more detail.

Analyse don't personalize

As I may already have said, there's no room for ego in teaching or forest school leading! In fact, as the consummate professionals we are, we are duty bound not to take things personally. Much as I might occasionally think, 'Do these kids know I've done a course? How dare they!', I'm never letting them know that! I aim never to let my emotions drive the decisions I make, and I always hide my buttons. If you don't, you can expect some children to push these buttons. Now,

I need to qualify this statement. If a learner says something offensive, perhaps it was a racist or sexist comment, you can bet I will have the necessary conversation. But no one is given a route map to my emotions. That would be silly.

If a young person's behaviour and comments are directed at me during forest school, I'll simply remain calm, and begin to analyse the behaviour in my head. I know this is easy to say; it is initially difficult, but eventually becomes second nature. I ask myself:

- What is the function of the behaviour? What need is being fulfilled? Is there a behaviour that has become habitual, because it has been successful?

- What is the context? Is there an audience and is this relevant? Is this an unfamiliar setting for the child? Have they been upset recently?

Once I understand the 'why' behind the behaviour, I'm in a far better position to deal with it, even if this analysis just tells me what not to do, as in this example:

A child has arrived at forest school, clearly not used to the woodland environment, and has had an upset with a number of other young people, who have subsequently laughed at her on the way to the fire area.

Leader: 'Good morning, everyone; welcome to our forest school!'
Child: 'I'm not staying here! You're stupid and so is forest school!'

Now, let's look at two contrasting responses. In the first, our leader reacts quickly, taking it personally:

Leader: 'Who do you think you're talking to, young lady?! You might get off with that at home, but you don't speak to me like that!'
Child: 'Don't you mention my home...'
Leader: 'I'll mention what I like...!'

You get the picture...

Now, let's say that in this next scenario, the leader manages to remind themselves that they are a skilled practitioner, well versed in the three mantras(!):

Leader (calmly analysing and seeing the heightened emotional state): '*I'm sorry you feel that way (smiles). It's fine for you to take a little time if you want to. When you're ready to join us, just pop into the fire circle, thanks.' (Smiles, gives a thumbs-up and engages with the other learners, to remove the audience and redirect attention.)*

Now, of course, this might not be the end of the situation. But clearly it's a signal that there's no conflict here – and it can't be worse than the 'how dare you?' approach. Equally, if my analysis tells me the child is looking to 'wind' me up, why on earth would I reinforce that behaviour by giving her what she wants? This route might serve to de-escalate many situations before they build up a head of steam; it might prevent the child from becoming overwhelmed; it certainly recognizes that the child's behaviour is likely to be in response to the emotional state caused by the earlier peer interactions, and perhaps a desire to be sent back to class/school. Will it work every time? Of course not, but we will have further ideas ready to use and we don't use a sledgehammer to crack a nut; we use the lightest touch possible to manage behaviour.

Fight fire with water

Our forest leader managed this well in the earlier scenario. I'll start by sharing with you a quote that stuck with me from training I attended years ago:

> In a conflict situation, the most mature participant takes the first opportunity to turn down the heat.

I love this. We are, of course, that person, if a child is behaving in a difficult or argumentative manner during a forest school session. Our role there is to de-escalate the situation, do it calmly and do nothing to cause escalation. Clearly in the previous scenario, you might struggle to be proactive; sometimes conflict can arise from nowhere, especially with complex cases. The behaviour is still functional and contextual remember, so you still do the analysis. Your awareness is high, you are giving the situation the appropriate level of attention, looking for signs of choice-driven belligerence – is the child looking for a way out of forest school? Why? Or are they in crisis mode? If so, what impact does that have on, for example, your body language choices or verbal responses? I will usually talk quietly, keep my tone friendly, maintain an appropriate level of eye contact – not so much that I get the 'stop staring at me' comment and not so little that I lower my perceived status in the learner's eyes. I might choose to sit down, pop my hands in my pockets, or display open, non-threatening body language, maybe carrying on with a chore or task I have been performing. All of these things suggest I am no threat, and I'm in control of myself and the situation.

I will use scripts, offer choices, ways out, or perhaps 'change face' with a colleague – anything to dampen down the flames, so to speak. The 'change face' technique works on the basis that, if the child is angry with me, and often too deep into this to be able to find a way out, I can create what we call a 'choice opportunity' by swapping with a colleague and letting them interact with the child while I move away. The child might not be emotionally able to calm if those emotions are directed at me, so we create a junction, a point where they can make a better choice, by changing the adult in front of them. The main issues with this occur when an adult's ego won't allow them to step away. So, leave your ego out of this!

And finally, as a wonderful behaviour ninja called Bob reminded me many years ago, when discussing this particular mantra, 'Just remember, Dave, not all fires can be put out with water. Some need a fire blanket or a chemical extinguisher, or foam.' A neat reminder that different approaches work for different children and young people, especially those designated as SEND. More on that later!

The problem is the problem, not the child

This is a crucial mantra to remember if we want to build effective working relationships with young people. We have to accept that we all make poor behaviour choices from time to time; it doesn't make us 'bad people'. We all know ourselves that when we are pushed beyond our normal coping threshold, we can react badly. This is true of everyone, but remember, your threshold might be considerably higher than many, if not all, of the learners who attend your forest school.

So, seek to separate the behaviour from the child. Help them to learn ways to manage better in the future. 'Bad' things, unfortunate events, can happen. What makes them especially sad is if we fail to learn something positive from such events. Don't miss these learning opportunities. Always look to help the learner to raise the bar for the next time, to delay the reaching of their threshold, to increase their resilience and equip them with coping strategies so that they are better able to avoid escalation next time, or at least delay it. Remember that, especially when working with complex cases or SEND, often the children who need our support, patience and guidance the most can appear (to the unaware) to deserve it the least...

These mantras, then, are part of that all-important perspective that will serve to underpin your practical approach and strategies, alongside the idea that we will try our utmost to be proactive rather than reactive. We will maintain the heightened level of awareness that the young people deserve and we will remain throughout firm, fair and friendly, within a framework that has a positive bias (of which I will talk later).

You may at this point be thinking, all well and good, but why bother thinking about perspective? Why not just have a list of strategies, explained for clarity, and ready to use tomorrow? (Don't worry, they're coming!) Well, you may have seen the wonderful pavement art which, when viewed from one angle, makes no sense at all, but when you stand in a certain spot, viewing from the right perspective, becomes a recognizable scene or character. Just do an internet search for 'perspective pavement art' and you'll see some great examples. Behaviour is like that; it's very easy to see what is on the surface and miss what is underneath. We are aiming to achieve behaviour ninja status, so that just won't do for us.

I mentioned that behaviour ninjas are proactive creatures by choice, equipped also with reactive strategies for the 'just in case' situations. Let's now explore how we can introduce that pre-emptive approach, nurture it, in us and in our forest school ethos. We need to kindle the flame so that the children attending our sessions will just seem, to the casual observer (and those looking to learn from you in the future), to 'behave' for you, even though the same children don't manage that for others. The secret? Routines...

Routines

Your aim is to establish the 'norms' of your forest school. It is possible these will resonate with the norms that the learners are used to in their classroom or the wider school, but that need not be the case. What I mean by that is that a group of children can be taught a whole new set of norms, if necessary. Don't be concerned that this will be confusing for them, as children and young people for the most part (with some notable exceptions we discuss later) are capable of adapting to circumstance, and we do them a disservice when we imagine they cannot. We will, of course, have strategies to support the more complex learners so that they can manage this more effectively.

It is useful to explore this notion of norms. Often teachers can explain the norms of their classroom, and then when I observe a few lessons, I find the learners communicating a whole different set of norms. Remember, the norms are, clearly, what is normal in your class (or forest school); what you allow on a regular basis; what the accepted behaviours, routines and practices are, as demonstrated regularly. Yes, other things may occasionally happen, out of the ordinary and therefore, by definition, they are not the norm. Try the exercise below:

1. Write a list of the norms you want for your forest school. Don't use vague terms like 'respect', or judgemental ones like 'good' or 'bad'. Talk in positive terms rather than letting it become a list of 'do not' rules. So, 'Do not run in the fire area' can be rephrased as 'We move slowly and carefully around the fire area.'

2. Compare this list with what usually happens! No judgement here, just be honest. Do the learners listen when others speak? Do they work within the physical boundaries you set out?

3. Where the two norms differ, we find our action points, the elements that need to change to achieve our desired and stated norms. These are the problems we will solve using suggestions in this book, so don't worry about them!

Routines are fundamental to this approach. These are practical ways in which the forest school will operate and will create desirable habits in the learners. You will already have some, for example, by going through the tool talks so that learners know we never walk around with an unsheathed knife, we use a saw safely, and so on. The way they enter the fire circle will be regulated also – perhaps there is a single entry point, perhaps they enter in a long line, walking round the outside of the area. Of course, if, three weeks into the term, you find you have relaxed these expectations and children are just wandering into the area as they wish, then the norm is just that. They haven't developed the habit you wanted.

Key point: When you establish a routine, you must intend to train the learners so it becomes habit, and reinforce it forever. Otherwise, the message you give to the young people is 'I have this rule, but you can safely ignore it, because you can be sure I will.' This is not the message we are looking for.

When you have come up with your routines, then you must embed them. At this point, the learning of the routines takes precedence over any other learning that is going on. Classroom teachers typically say to me, 'How do I have time for this stuff when I have a curriculum to deliver?' In truth, if you don't establish and embed your routines thoroughly, and make them habit, then you'll find yourself spending more time throughout the year doing this and dealing with issues that needn't have occurred otherwise. So take the time now to embed routines and say, 'These are my *permanent* expectations.' Forest school leaders might say that they are more interested in the learner-led approach, and as it is the foundation of forest school, won't routines stifle this? Remember, we are establishing our routines for behaviour, so that we create an environment that enables learners to lead, not prevent it. In that way, our behaviour routines are no different to equipping learners with tool skills. You wouldn't leave the children to a learner-led approach to using a knife, would you?

I have worked with young people who have all been arrested for knife-related offences. Early on in their forest school experiences, I clearly needed to establish routines about knife use. A knife could not have the unhealthy draw that it had held previously with this group. We therefore developed a routine to embed the idea that they needed to see it as a tool. We made no great drama about introducing knives; it was matter-of-fact. We called it a bladed tool, never a knife. It was kept in a 'toolbox'. We used it for tasks then put it away; not even just sheathing it and carrying it but putting it in the box. This was the routine and we reinforced it every time, without exception. It might sound tedious, and perhaps it was, but we did it ourselves, we led by example, gently reminding the young people of the expectation; we didn't make a huge fuss, as we wanted it to be 'just what we do' with this tool, rather than, 'It's a knife! We might get cut!' It became the norm we wanted it to be, the novelty value of the knife was diminished and its value as a tool was established.

I'm not suggesting that you all need to do this; few of us will be working with this extreme of behaviour, but it does serve to illustrate the power of embedding a routine, and reinforcing this with a consistent message – we practise what we preach. When these teenagers decided they would like to build a shelter, or a bridge across the stream, they still had those learner-led opportunities, beloved and nurtured by good leaders everywhere, but they were also able to safely use knives, where previously they could not.

We have now looked at our underpinning, supportive philosophy and perspective. Exploring routines and norms, we now know the importance of establishing and embedding our ethos with those who attend our forest school. Now let's get down to the 'nitty gritty'. We will explore named strategies, some that are useful proactively, others reactively and still others that can be used, with some adaptation, in both ways. We will explore these with examples; you might need to think further about how you could adapt them to your needs, to suit the age group you work with and their specific needs and context. These adaptations are numerous and would fill volumes were I to attempt to cover all possibilities. That is where your local knowledge must work in your favour. We all like being given the space to use our professional judgement and these strategies I hope will always leave room for you to be able to do that. Read on!

Chapter 6

TECHNIQUES YOU CAN USE TOMORROW IN YOUR FOREST SCHOOL

Develop a positive bias

The underpinning ideas behind this are discussed elsewhere within this book. Suffice to say that one of the most important truths of behaviour management, regardless of age, SEND and so on, is that we get more of the kind of behaviour we focus on. When I was supporting a school in the north of England, a Year 11 girl once said to me, 'The most important thing we do here is misbehave.' I thought this a remarkable statement (sometimes you just know you've got to dig deeper), and so I asked her to justify that comment. She said, 'Well, that's what all the teachers notice.' This was an epiphany moment! Let's choose to focus on good behaviour – we want more of it. Here are some examples of how you can demonstrate a positive bias at forest school:

- Tell children what you want them to do, rather than telling them to stop an undesirable behaviour. For example: 'Michaela! Stop running around the fire area!' could be: 'Michaela! We walk in the fire area' or, 'Michaela! How could you be safer in the fire area?'

Note I've left the exclamation mark, to show that we can avoid the 'stop' comments even in situations relating to safety.

- Notice positives. You need to achieve a ratio here, where positive to negative comments are, as a minimum five to one. This is just a start until you are proficient. Plan this; be determined to notice those getting it right: 'Robert, Bolu, Simon, well done. You are all using your saws safely, the way we showed you.'

- Use 'proximity praise' and 'catch them being good', two techniques that are great examples of a positive bias. Let's imagine you notice one child chatting while you wait for attention from the group. You then praise those who are displaying the desired behaviour (proximity praise): 'Sharmaine, Laura, you are giving me your attention, thanks. Peter, you too, that's good to see.' When the inattentive child sees this and alters their behaviour, you notice that positive too, and praise them (catch them being good). Perhaps if a child shouts out an answer, and there is a 'hands-up' expectation and routine in place, identify a different child who has followed the routine, 'Orla, thank you for following the hands-up routine. What's the answer?' Even if the 'shouter' was right, never, ever say, 'Well Katie, we don't shout out, but yes, you're right.' That tells the group that your expectations, routines and norms are open to abuse. I also like the 'Steal it!' approach. So if a child shouts out a correct answer, I'll respond with 'Steal it!' and hands will shoot up to pinch the answer. It can have a rapid impact on shouting out!

Anticipate compliance

This is a technique teachers have borrowed and adapted from sales people; what they often call the Assumed Close. Even if you don't know this named technique, there's a very good chance that it has been used on you! This is when the salesperson says to you, 'OK, so how many can I put you down for?' Not, 'Do you want this?' but, 'You can't not want this, in fact, you need several!' In your forest school, this is a valuable technique because it is the behaviour of a 'high-status person'. You must be that. Sometimes a teaching assistant or new teacher might have the role of forest school leader. Some children might perceive such people as low status (most TAs have heard the comment, 'You're not a teacher') and that needs to change. If you are an outside forest school provider coming into the school to facilitate the learning, children will not necessarily see you as an authority figure, so you must develop your status in their eyes. High-status people are calm and measured. Anticipating compliance demonstrates this. You can utilize this technique by issuing an instruction, then thanking them in advance, and shifting your focus elsewhere; it's a done deal, so why would you need to linger? Take this example, where perhaps the children have decided they'd like to make a nature display:

The forest school leader sees a learner who is not engaged with their group, who are collecting interesting items from the woodland floor to bring back to the fire area for discussion. Instead, he is snapping branches from a sapling, so we can hardly be happy just to let this youngster learn in their own way:

'Nathan! Stop doing that! Why aren't you helping the group?'

Nathan kicks the ground, shoving his hands in his pockets. 'Cos it's boring! I'm not picking up stupid pine cones!'

'Nathan! That's very rude! Don't speak to me like that...'

This is not great and has the potential to escalate... Instead, we would always first be curious about the behaviour, then we can pick a more effective response. In many cases, a better way to deal with this is to anticipate compliance:

The forest school leader sees a learner who is not engaged with their group, who are collecting interesting items from the woodland floor to bring back to the fire area for discussion.

'Nathan, see if you can find at least three different natural items, and maybe one man-made item. I bet you can. Thanks!' The leader smiles, gives him a thumbs-up, then turns to speak to another child.

This leader has cleverly used the technique, but also added a positive comment and the thumbs-up and by turning away shows a further expectation that Nathan will do as he has been directed. If there was any debate, it's over.

This works for belligerent youngsters, younger children as well as those older learners who might be rewarded by drawing you into a debate. For SEND children and those with complex needs, it is a valid technique, for example for children who display conduct disorder (CD), who can display quite manipulative and calculating behaviour, and seek out conflict.

Be curious about behaviour!

Remember, behaviour is both functional and contextual; it has a purpose and is often specific to environment, audience and so on, so finding the 'why' behind the behaviour is crucially important. I once heard a great quote: 'Understanding is hard. Once we understand, action is easy.'[1] It is a truth of behaviour that five children might display identical behaviour for five different reasons. Consider this situation: you are organizing the group to go out to the forest school area. Five children are not following the instruction to line up smartly at the door:

Child 1 is doing this because someone in the class was nasty to them in the yard earlier.

---

1   Chinese statesman, physician and political philosopher Sun Yat-sen (1866–1925).

Child 2 is reluctant because he is scared of wasps and there are a few in the forest area.

Child 3 does not like adults controlling him. He has a diagnosis of pathological demand avoidance (PDA).

Child 4 arrived late to school because his mum and dad had a row in the car on the way. He's feeling anxious about it.

Child 5 hasn't heard you! He's usually really keen to get to forest school where he gets to burn off excess energy!

It might be that you'll struggle to find a 'one size fits all' solution to this, and perhaps need a combination of a few techniques. The point is, the function of the behaviour, and the context in which it is happening, is different for each child. Knowing that is useful. Incidentally, in this scenario, I'd be looking to use a countdown, interspersed with praise, reassurance and perhaps a 'when/then' script, to manage this situation (more on those later).

Scripts

Scripted responses are a much-valued tool among educators dealing with challenging behaviour. They can be used for repetitive, predictable issues as well as those curve balls that learners can throw your way. They help you to remain calm, in control and therefore perceived as high status. A typical example to demonstrate what I mean would be the aforementioned 'when/then' script beloved of many teachers around the globe!

'Miss, I want to go to forest school now, not after break!'
    *'John, **when** we have completed our morning maths activity, **then** we can go to the forest site, thanks.'*

It's easy to see that this kind of script creates a scaffold and you simply fill in the gaps. It means that you can think as you speak and always seem to have an answer. Remaining calm and always having an answer is the behaviour of a high-status person. Equally, a script can sit as a stand-alone sentence, as a starter to a sentence, or a closing comment. For example:

- Stand-alone script: 'You can follow my instructions or you can choose to accept the consequences.'

- Scripted start: 'Himesh? Himesh, I need you to...', followed by instructions. The script consists of using the name twice to ensure attention before the instruction is repeated.

- Scripted finish: 'Ellie, you did well yesterday; that's the Ellie I'd like to see in forest school today, thanks.' This follows a correction of undesirable behaviour.

- Remember, a stand-alone script can be developed for situations you've never come across even though we usually generate scripts for situations that we know will happen. So, I have a 'get out' script for situations that have come out of the blue: 'I'm not going to discuss this now, thanks. We will talk about it/deal with it later.'

You can see that there are millions of possible scripts, but they are so powerful for anyone managing behaviour. Scripts for forest school are easy; after all, tool talks are nothing but an expanded version of a script, and we've all learned those. See the use of a choice script in the following scenario:

Molly is waving a stick she has burned in the fire; sparks from the fire are landing in areas we don't want them.

Even the most die-hard advocate of the learner leading the learning would find it hard to explain to a parent why they allowed this behaviour to continue, resulting in a burn. So, let's intervene:

'Molly, you can use that stick to toast a marshmallow, or you can put it in the fire and move away, thank you.' (Note: usually with a choice script of this type, it seems to pay to speak the choice that is most desirable to you first, before the alternative.)

Adapted 'meet and greet' technique

Most teachers will know the meet and greet technique, which is a terrific, assertive approach that oozes high status. In simple terms, a teacher meets the group at the door of the class, and they are trained (just like any other routine) to wait quietly and calmly and enter when instructed to do so, on the teacher's terms. It's a positive experience, though, since the teacher gets to meet and speak to every child.

Adapted for forest school, you can gather the group at the class, or wherever, so that they set off according to your expectations (and not before). Or you can wait for them at the entrance to forest school. This is not meant to crush their enjoyment at coming to the woods, or their need to run free! I'm suggesting that this is a technique you might select for a challenging group. Alternatively – and this is how I prefer to do things, purely because it suits the forest school site I use – I allow them ten minutes' free play, call them to the fire area (which has a huge green parachute suspended above it), meet and greet them in the area (they'll have left their bags by the store area so they collect these after free play) and then they take their seats.

Why bother with meet and greet? Well, you stake your claim as leader. You present yourself as assertive. But it's more than that. You present them with a threshold to cross. Once crossed, there are routines and expectations. Equally, you get to greet each child positively. You can gauge how they're feeling, remind them of previous sessions where they were brilliant, calm those who haven't managed it themselves, reinforce expectations with those who are a little inattentive, and nip issues in the bud. You're solving behaviour before it happens, like those ninjas we discussed earlier...

Some people like to shake hands, give high fives and so on, but that's up to you. For certain a smile for each child is an investment you can draw on later. Remember too, for some children, sadly, you might be the first, indeed the only, adult to smile at them that day...

Adapted secret student

I first saw this technique, I believe, on Teachers' TV and instantly loved it, so thanks to whoever came up with it. It is wonderfully simple and a doddle to adapt for forest school. Perhaps you can change the name to 'woodland wonder' or something else that suits. Let me first explain the technique; I've used it to great effect in class and forest school, and with Year 3 children, home education groups, 15-year-old lads at risk of exclusion, and SEND groups. It works!

First, you decide which learner is the secret student or woodland wonder. You don't tell them who it is; you simply say someone has been chosen. You tell the group that, if the woodland wonder shows the kind of behaviour we expect (you'll already have made this clear, but perhaps the question 'Can anyone here tell me exactly the behaviour we like to notice?' will be worthwhile), then they will earn something towards a reward planned for the end of term/end of session, depending on needs. I use arrows on the board in class which I colour in as they progress towards a finish line; in the woods, perhaps have an outline picture of an animal, or an outline of a tree, the shape spilt into segments, so that you can colour them in, until the whole outline is filled. I use this over an extended period so there is a visual representation of their progress.

This technique is good because it takes an issue and makes it a solution, and that's a great way for a behaviour manager to view issues. I use it particularly when a group tends to feed off each other, and behaviour issues escalate as bravado and one-upmanship take over. The problem, when we ask the 'Why?' question (Why is this behaviour occurring? What is its function and context?), is that they care what their peers think. This is currently manifesting as poor behaviour choices through negative peer influence. The solution? Make the peer influence a good thing! Let's say two or three learners are displaying poor behaviour choices. You then mention to the group generally, 'I wonder if the woodland wonder is behaving well?' You then get learners whispering to those who are not managing their behaviour, encouraging them to 'behave'. Positive peer influence!

So, you've told them you've chosen a woodland wonder. What now? Well, you can use (not overuse) it subtly, as above, throughout the day to help learners make better choices. You can, at the end of the day, name and praise the woodland wonder if they did well, which can boost their self-esteem and help if they have low status in the group. What if the woodland wonder has not done well? You don't name them, crucially, but you use your prepared script (of course): 'Unfortunately, the woodland wonder has not behaved in the way we expect, so I can't colour any parts in. But most of you behaved so well, I'm sure the next woodland wonder will do great!' No big fuss, no guilt trip, no looking daggers at anyone. Keep it positive! Because you haven't named the person, every child has to reflect on their behaviour choices – which is what we want, right? Some children will want to ask if they were the woodland wonder but this is predictable, so you'll have a script; something like, 'Don't worry, let's just focus on next time – I know we'll do better!'

Any other potential obstacles? If a child was woodland wonder last session, they might think they are safe to take risks during this one. Solution? Early in the process, make one child the woodland wonder twice in a row. Some children might enjoy the sabotage of this process, especially some complex cases. Solution? Remove them from the equation. They'll still have the usual interventions, including sanctions (we'll talk about these later), especially if the behaviour is choice-driven. We know, of course, that in some cases children can't always help that they don't meet our behaviour expectations, and at that point, punishment via consequences would not be the most effective choice, and certainly not the fairest. What if a child has put huge efforts into trying all day – perhaps they are diagnosed as having attention deficit hyperactivity disorder (ADHD) and have managed their impulsivity brilliantly in the hope that they are the woodland wonder or secret student? At times like this, I simply change who the named person is halfway through the day!

Gimmicks like this can have a remarkable effect on problem groups, including those of whom colleagues might say, 'No, I wouldn't take those kids into a forest!' However, it is valid with 'good' groups too (i.e., those who find their needs met wonderfully well by the ethos and activities of forest school, and do not seem to need anything else). It can work as a 'maintainer', and we should not take good behaviour choices for granted. Poor choices can creep in by increments. In the arena of mountain safety (I am a keen hiker), the angle of a slope can creep upwards degree by degree without causing untoward concern. However, when it reaches 38 degrees, that is the angle at which an avalanche becomes possible. Behaviour is like that too; it can gradually change to the point where an 'avalanche' occurs. So let's not get there!

If you are unsure about the impact of secret student/woodland wonder, try this technique, which can illustrate how impactful gimmicks can be. When the children arrive, tell them you've chosen five of them at random to receive a call/email/message home tonight to talk about their behaviour at forest school today. Again, they aren't named. You simply say you're expecting to make five very positive calls, but you will make whatever calls are necessary, so it's about the choices they make. Then see how it goes. It's rarely let me down but I have to say, if it does, I make the tough calls too, in as positive a way as I can! With this technique, I don't reveal the five names; they wait until they get home. And I never fail to make the calls... That would be the most terrible message I could give the learners, wouldn't it?

Repair and reconnect

There will be times, inevitably, when you need to correct or challenge the behaviour choices of learners at your forest school. This can tax relationships you might have been working long and hard to establish. Of course, positive working relationships with young people can be judged by how well they stand up to such situations, but still we can do a lot to minimize the damage, in the way we choose to correct behaviour (firmly and fairly). We can also follow up with the repair and reconnect technique, which is brilliant for complex cases. I've used it with learners with attachment issues, ADHD learners, and youngsters with CD and autism spectrum disorder (ASD).

At its heart is the message, 'The behaviour choice was the problem, I still like and value you.' Therefore, very soon after I have needed to challenge a learner about their behaviour, I reconnect with them. This lets them know there are no hard feelings (as indeed there should not be; that would be a case of bearing a grudge, and as professionals we cannot do that). Let us say then, that we find ourselves in the following situation:

Taylor has become over-excited during free play. Rather than throw the willow rings towards the pegs he should be aiming at, he's throwing them at other learners. You've asked him to take time out at his sit spot to reflect, and your colleague followed up two minutes later with a conversation that led to Taylor apologizing to the others. However, he is still glancing apprehensively towards you.

'Taylor, do you want to help me gather some tools for our next activity?'

Now, if you are concerned Taylor could sulk, refuse, or disengage (and you will know if this is the case far better than I...) then you might choose to phrase it differently:

'Taylor, I could do with some help from you if you are feeling up to it.'

Then, turning away, head for the tool area. As mentioned earlier, this is high-status behaviour. Also, you've left choice with the learner, so it would be useful if Taylor were resistant to adult control, perhaps with a diagnosis of PDA or oppositional defiant disorder (ODD).

From this, you can see that you can easily use a technique like repair and reconnect, adapting it according to the individual's needs. Of course, finding strategies to enable you to better support children with diagnosed conditions can be challenging, but as we become accustomed to this level of awareness, it doesn't have to mean a huge level of additional work for us.

Take-up time

This is another high-status behaviour technique. Far too often, teachers will make a demand of a child, then stand, hands on hips, waiting for the learner to follow it. This might be accompanied by a stern expression, and even comments that do not help, such as, 'Well, then? Come on! I'm waiting!' This might sound like good old-fash-ioned behaviour management to some people. Well, it certainly is old-fashioned! Possibly Victorian. It might sound like the norm in many schools, and sadly, this might be true. It usually works for the children who don't need to be spoken to like that. But with complex cases and SEND? Or children with low resilience? Or those who are timid, anxious, and so on? Definitely not useful. Far better, then, to give a child or young person take-up time. It can make an instruction far more palatable to them. For example:

Taylor goes to his sit spot to reflect. Your colleague gives him time to do this, then approaches him. Rather than stand over him, she cleverly sits down close by.

'Taylor, I'm sure you've thought sensibly about what happened. When you're ready – not now – I will be sitting by the fire; I just need to keep it going ready for lunch. Pop over and let me know how you'd like to make things better.'

Much better than demanding an apology, wouldn't you agree?

Proximity praise

This is a great technique, which I've used with my own children, with primary, secondary and SEND groups, from many backgrounds. It works in class, it works in the woods, it's brilliant! It keeps the positive bias going. We've already seen it in action earlier, but to reiterate: proximity praise works by you noticing children who are doing well, specifically in an attempt to help another child make a better behaviour choice than they are currently. Obviously, when there is a safety issue, this would be unsuitable! Unsafe behaviour needs to stop right away, and subtle goes out of the window.

Remember also that in forest school, child-led learning can be a regular, wonderful element of what we do, and can potentially form the bulk of a session for most children. I might be very careful about using this technique for what might be seen as 'daydreaming' or 'off-task behaviour' in a classroom!

That being said, look at the example below:

The children have set up an impromptu obstacle course around the woodland area, and are enjoying using it. However, Carly is pushing in front of others, not being polite, and upsetting one or two learners.

Leader: 'John, Omar, Lola, you are playing so well. You're being patient, taking turns and being kind. That's great forest school behaviour, well done.' These children are close to Carly. She hears this, and goes to the back of the queue.

Leader: 'Carly, well done, that's polite behaviour too.'

Our leader followed up proximity praise with the catch them being good technique when Carly conformed to our norms. This reinforces the behaviour we want more of.

PPTV (pace, pitch, tone, volume of voice)

I include this technique here because, when I'm coaching individual teachers, support staff and forest leaders, it is one of the most common things we address early on, and can have an amazing impact. Additionally, the atmosphere of a forest school can be loud, high energy and busy, but the leader who presents as calm, fun and approachable is remembered. So the PPTV of the leader's voice is absolutely critical.

There are no 'perfect' levels for this; it is a dynamic thing dependent on the situation and character of the leader. Generally, I feel it works best for me when I go for slowing my speech down, dropping the pitch a little, keeping my tone friendly (becoming especially determined about, and aware of this when poor behaviour occurs) and I like to keep the volume down, unless circumstances dictate otherwise (safety). If I have a noisy group, I don't get louder. I drop the volume, choosing to almost whisper, so they have to actively listen. I might use a raised hand signal for when I need attention, so I raise my hand, and the children copy this when they see me. It quickly spreads through the group. I have even used a Buddhist singing bowl[2] to get attention, which works brilliantly.

Adding a further element to this, it is vital to monitor your facial expression too. I'm never sure whether face influences tone, or the other way around, but it doesn't matter – your facial expression can certainly influence the young person, and a quick internet search will give you a range of research data about how much. One set of statistics I feel fits – and it's by no means the highest – is this. When we are communicating with someone:

- 55 per cent of that communication is through facial expression and body language

- 38 per cent is tone of voice

- 7 per cent is the words we say.[3]

A measly 7 per cent! So, be critically aware of your facial expression.

---

2   Typically a copper or brass bowl, struck with a wooden mallet to emit a deeply resonant hum which aids relaxation and a sense of calm.

3   Albert Mehrabian's 7–38–55 Rule of Personal Communication.

Relaxing the facial muscles will also make you feel more relaxed, and remember, that's when we make our best decisions.

Conclusion

These techniques are by no means the only ones you could use and there are a great many good books on behaviour management out there, although none that are specific to forest school, as I write! I always tell people who work with children to become curious about behaviour; read extensively, copy, adapt and blend techniques that you find so that they work for you (the use of sales speak with the anticipate compliance technique is a great example of this). After all, one of the things we often do as educators is to seem as if we've known forever that fact which we only learned yesterday. The same can most certainly apply to the techniques we are discussing here!

Chapter 7

SUPPORTING SEND BEHAVIOUR IN YOUR FOREST SCHOOL

Attention deficit hyperactivity disorder (ADHD)

I have witnessed looks of horror and disbelief on the faces of teachers when I have explained that yes, I am going to take the 'ADHD kids' into the woods. Yes, the very same children are going to make fire, use sharp things, have some dreaded child-directed time, wander, and maybe even do some archery. No (I tell them), I'm not concerned that the children have 'issues' of impulsivity, lack of attention, an inability to concentrate on a task for an extended period. Because, you see, the outdoors is often therapy for these children. It is a fundamental need, in my opinion, and to deny them the opportunity is like denying any other potentially beneficial intervention to someone who needs it. Another reason I'm not concerned is that I have taken account of needs in my approach and any planning I have done. I'm being proactive.

I run a course for ADHD learners. This is not pure forest school; in fact, only small amounts of time are unstructured in terms of activities, at least initially. This being said, we do find that the learn-ers can choose the content of their day as we progress. And remem-ber, these children are the ones who frequently find themselves 'risk assessed' out of outdoor opportunities.

I've had referrals from schools, parents and psychologists. The course consists usually of about six full days, over a UK half-term of schooling, for one day a week. It takes place outdoors, in the woods. The content is not set in stone, for two main reasons: first, I don't know where the group might lead me, and second, there are seasonal variations I like to take advantage of. The course is called The Hunter Gatherer. My colleague and I take the group on a journey into our Mesolithic past. They learn the skills of our ancestors, as they would have been towards the end of that period, where they were moving through an endless woodland landscape, rich with opportunity, wan-dering from place to place according to seasonal food sources. We do not actually hunt, for obvious reasons, but we process foods and cook them on the fire. This could be meat, fish, berries, eggs. They process and eat nettles. They learn a few basic traps (with strict rules about never using them practically) and they always learn to track, no matter the season. Tracking is the art of reading signs that helps us to know what has gone on, which animal has been here and where it's most likely to have gone after that. ADHD children are frequently brilliant at it. You might think that sounds strange and this view could be justified; after all, being able to track can require focus and concentration for extended periods. Not qualities we would normally attribute to ADHD learners, right?

Well, experience over many years has taught me otherwise. I have found that ADHD learners in the outdoors are different from their classroom selves. Over the years, I have heard teachers many times say, 'He's just a different person out here.' Then two things happened for me, at approximately the same time, that had a pro-found effect on me. I watched a TEDx Talk about ADHD, delivered by a doctoral student (diagnosed with ADHD), entitled 'ADHD sucks, but not really'. And I bought a book by Thom Hartmann, entitled *ADHD:*

A Hunter in a Farmer's World. These were fortunate finds for me. They reminded me of a comment I once heard from an educational psychologist who, talking about ADHD learners, said, 'The educational tide has gone out, and left ADHD kids floundering on the sand.' I suppose, from an evolutionary perspective, the classroom is an alien environment for us all...

So, the course was based on this idea. It seems that the set of behaviours we have labelled as ADHD may have been part of human genetic makeup for thousands and thousands of years. In a hunter-gatherer society, they are a positive; in a 'civilized' world (and classroom), perhaps not. For example, we all know ADHD learners can get distracted – the teacher is at the front of the class, performing their role, firing on all cylinders (hopefully), delivering an awesome, engaging lesson, and suddenly the 'ADHD kid' notices something outside the window, maybe bellows, 'Squirrel!,' and the room descends into chaos. But...that bias towards peripheral movement that causes the outburst is useful in a hunter-gatherer situation. These are the first people to notice the edible mushroom tucked away on the track edge. They see the deer as it is startled from a scrape where it has been lying low. In hunter societies (including those that exist today), perhaps they are first to fire an arrow, maybe felling the deer and feeding the clan. They have high status because of this, in the eyes of their fellows. But not in the classroom...

You may have noticed something that seems a little strange about the behaviour of a child who is identified as having an attention deficit. They can sometimes become extremely focused on a single task or item, often at the expense of all else. This can make moving on to another task quite frustrating for a classroom-based teacher, but can it be useful in other contexts? Well, let's say the hunter fires the arrow, but misses or wounds the prey, which then takes off through the undergrowth. Now the hunter must switch (and crucially, is motivated to do so) from peripheral focus to focus on details as they track the animal, needing to spot footprints, but also overturned stones, impressions in bent grass blades and so on. As I thought about all this, my experiences with ADHD children, some of which have puzzled me for years, suddenly made sense. Perspective matters, of course. Now, it's possible that in ten years' time, someone may argue a different theory and that's fine, but right now, this works for me and is currently the best way I have of understanding ADHD learners so that I can support them effectively.

So, what *can* we do for ADHD learners through forest school? Well, I'm not asking you to dress them in skins and start making stone tools (although we do...and they are good at that too!). Let's keep it within the practical possibilities of a standard forest school. First though, let's take a brief overview.

Attention deficit hyperactivity disorder is a condition affecting brain development, impacting on attention, the ability to sit still for extended periods, and self-regulation. Direct focus is a struggle for these children. Some learners may be predominantly inattentive, some may be hyperactive/impulsive, and others a (heady) combination of both. There is often co-morbidity with ODD, CD and other issues. The ADHD brain seems to find novelty stimulating (great for a seasonally shifting hunter-gatherer). This could explain the drive behind the ADHD child who throws the rubber in class and sits back while the resultant uproar occurs.

MANAGING ATTENTION DEFICIT HYPERACTIVITY DISORDER IN FOREST SCHOOL

- Let nature do its thing! There is substantial evidence from many sources to suggest that nature can support attentional functioning. Most people who enjoy time in the woods know this. Direct attention gives way to an involuntary version; we enjoy a view, for example, or birdsong from the thicket nearby. It doesn't require the effort that direct attention (required in class) does. 'Green play' is good for us all.

- Be brave! Include free play, child led, in their forest school menu. Yes, some adult 'nudging' may be required, but recognize when that soft fascination for what they are doing kicks in, and nurture it.

- Play to their strengths! I want ADHD learners to celebrate their 'ADHD-ness'. I call it 'hunter traits' on my course (their chests swell with pride), not ADHD. Who wants a label with 'deficit' and 'disorder' in it?! If a footprint in the mud, or the way the wind is shifting, or a bird's nest in the brambles becomes interesting to them, spend some time on it.

- Give them a project they can revisit over several weeks, when it suits them (remember, forest school should be a long-term intervention). This could be, for example, creating their own bird feeders, replenishing them, perhaps setting up a hide, recording findings and so on.

- Allow, within the boundaries of your risk/benefit analysis, activities like climbing, throwing at a target, building and digging. Perhaps they can dig a ground oven, to learn how hunter societies of today still cook food. It could resemble the Maori 'hangi' oven used by indigenous New Zealanders. Again, I'm not saying you have to plan to do this, just that you should seize the opportunity when it arises naturally, recognizing the value to an ADHD learner (and, of course, most children will love this).

- In your interactions, maintain that firm, fair, friendly approach. If you give instructions to the group, occasionally ask the ADHD learners to repeat them back, to check for understanding – not always those children only, of course. Make sure you praise the ADHD learner in public, and if a correction or admonishment is necessary, then it is best done privately.

- Movement breaks can help an ADHD child to self-regulate, and are so much easier to manage in forest school, although in a day full of variety they may not even be needed. The ADHD brain seems to be driven by a need to seek novelty, and there's lots of that inherent in forest school. You might in some cases agree to a signal between you and the child which can be used if either of you feels a movement break would help with impulse control or self-regulation. This signal is pre-arranged and you must ensure the child uses it respectfully. I worked with a child who had ADHD and used the phrase, 'Do you need my support?' to help him stay on task. If he continued to struggle, I would switch to '(Name), you need support.' That was the signal to come to me, and I'd refocus with him, or he'd take a movement break. Eventually, he'd hear the signal phrase and take off on a movement break! Some studies show that 20 minutes of nature can generate a couple of hours of newly 'rebooted' focus and attention. I do know a school which allows ADHD learners a movement break before they step into their final exams – brilliant!

- Sometimes a 'study buddy' can be beneficial to an ADHD learner. They often seem to raise the bar on their attention span, which of course we want to support them to do. The study buddy needs to have the attributes of calmness, maturity and responsibility. See if you can utilize this approach in your forest school, perhaps with paired tasks. Once again, that doesn't mean you have to deliberately plan paired tasks, just that you can encourage pairing when they come up with their own ideas.

- Perspective is important! No child is simply a label and there is a lot more that goes into the complex individual who arrives in your forest school than 'just' ADHD. But there are times when ADHD learners cannot help that they 'won't do it'. I like to think of those with a diagnosis of ADHD not as inattentive but as 'differently attentive'.

- Approach tool use with caution. This would apply to ADHD from a point of view of impulsivity and inattentiveness. Teach them to focus; teach this element very clearly, with lots of observed practice.

Conduct disorder (CD)

This is potentially a very complex disorder, presenting real challenges. This is one of those cases where we do ourselves a favour by defining the word 'challenging' as 'difficult, but stimulating'! I have worked with CD learners for almost three decades now, and for me, keeping our level of awareness high is crucial; remember, as we should with many complex issues, that children and young people with CD will often find their lives made even more of a challenge by the reactions they get from others, including professionals. We need to take pride in our ability to see the person behind the condition, to separate the two, and look to nurture the positive traits that the child will undoubtedly have and that are often well hidden. Children with CD are definitely in that category of youngsters who can make it hard for people to like them, unless that awareness is there. This is a sad fact.

I have worked in the outdoors many times with CD learners, undertaking 'traditional' activities like canoeing and climbing, as well as bushcraft and forest school, even residentials. CD learners should not be excluded from such opportunities. Do your risk assessment, put in the necessary measures, and remember that the experience could be a pivotal one for them and for your relationship with them.

Identification (not your job) and multi-faceted intervention at an early stage can be the most effective elements of treatment. Children with CD are 'high risk'. Dropping out of education is a possibility and often follows lots of disciplinary action and sporadic truancy. They can also develop into risk takers, involving anything from wandering off as a young child, to drug taking and other criminal activity as they get older. However, we can play an important role, as outdoor educators, in helping young people to overcome this condition.

With CD, we see a range of behavioural and emotional issues that are repetitive and persistent. Serious misbehaviour can include aggression towards adults, resistance to adult control, manipulation, intimidation and lying. As mentioned, it can develop into more serious issues, including criminal activity. Most behaviour seen with CD would be described as anti-social but it is helpful for us to see the behaviours as anxiety driven. Interactions with peers can be fraught with issues, and some peers might feel intimidated by the conduct disordered child. Additional conditions can include ADHD and post-traumatic stress disorder.

MANAGING CONDUCT DISORDER IN FOREST SCHOOL

- The inherent qualities of the outdoor environment may well help, but be aware that your risk assessment will need to factor in the possibility of the child breaching the site boundaries you have set. I have a generic CD risk assessment and back this up if required (often!) with another, specific to the child.

- Build the relationship slowly, particularly with older learners. I find that if I am overly positive with them initially, they can perceive that as a weakness. Therefore, I prefer to keep older CD learners guessing a little. I keep emotional reactions to positive behaviour fairly low key, genuine and sincere, and don't dwell on them. This is because CD learners can react negatively to praise. I might develop their praise acceptance and our effective working relationship by using a technique called triangulated praise. I praise them to their parent/carer/teacher, knowing it will filter back to them. I also use remote praise, where I might praise them to another learner or a colleague, within their hearing but without directly acknowledging them. This is a fantastic technique with CD, and indeed, with any learner who is not comfortable with direct, public praise (with or without a diagnosis).

- If a learner cannot follow your routines, then those routines may need to become rules for them specifically. You must support them with this and aim to help them make better choices, but you must also have some system of sanctions. With sanctions, remember that they should be certain, not severe. So, if a child persists in breaching the physical boundaries (a routine expectation), then they can find themselves having a higher level of supervision imposed, time out (a short period; 'time in' is better than 'time out', I feel, because it gives input and support from an adult when it's needed, rather than isolation), or even, ultimately, removal from forest school. I try to avoid this; if I have to use it, it is usually for a short period. The most effective sanction I have used, in all honesty, is removal of my attention for a short period. It's not a huge thing, but the certainty is what can make it matter.

- Activities, chosen by children or planned, that build in positive social interaction can be beneficial because their often-negative behaviour can make their peers distance themselves from CD children. If you can get to the position where a CD child is a successful secret student or woodland wonder, this is very positive!

- Issuing instructions can be complex. 'You need to saw that log for the fire' might result in refusal. 'The fire needs more fuel; can you help me out?' might be more effective. Also use variations of the choice script. 'Would you like red or black gloves while using the saw?' will still get the work done (the sawing), but the choice is left with the child (colour of gloves).

- Teach the right behaviours! This is as important as teaching practical skills in the outdoors, or the curriculum in the classroom. I might give learners simple tasks around the fire, but they know I'm watching for them following the 'calm around the campfire' routine. Remember, the completion of the tasks is of secondary importance in this case.

- Embed all routines from day one; they must seem 'normal'. This structure is important to all young people but crucial to CD learners.

- Seek to reward positive behaviour, but be aware of the individual. Can they cope with public praise, or does it need to be a surreptitious smile and thumbs-up, or a quiet word one to one later?

- Maintain high expectations of these learners and once relationships are positive, use this (unashamedly) to your advantage. CD children are part of that complex group that will follow you, long before they follow any notion of rules.

Oppositional defiant disorder (ODD)

This is another disorder that can be wrapped up with social, emotional and mental health (SEMH) issues. It is another one of the conditions where the learner's issues are further complicated and exacerbated by how they present, causing negative reactions in the unaware. The outward signs can be quite stigmatizing, often put down to 'bad' parenting, and mean that professionals and peers of the child find them tough to like. In fact, while parenting can improve the management of ODD as well as exacerbate the issues, there is a lot more to it than that and there are a number of possible causes, including genetics and brain injury. However, we should recognize that an unstable family life, with perhaps regular disputes, substance abuse, general disharmony, inconsistency, bereavement and loss are hardly situations where we can lay blame at the child's door, and the prevalence of these issues in the lives of ODD children suggests that we can provide support by exposing ODD learners to alternative perspectives. These might include kindness, consistency, emotional stability and healthy living, to name a few, and all are easily done through forest school. As a note of caution, though, I have met young people diagnosed with ODD who came from stable and loving homes. So we should worry less about 'how they got where they are' and more about how to support them to move to where they want (and need) to be. Remember, this is a treatable disorder and it needn't be lifelong.

With ODD learners, the behaviours you might typically see include regular temper tantrums, most of which can seem to come 'out of the blue', or occur over seemingly trivial matters. This can be accompanied by spite and revenge-seeking with peers, belligerence towards adults, refusing to follow, or persistently questioning rules, being 'deliberately' annoying and having an external locus of control (it's always someone else's fault).

MANAGING OPPOSITIONAL DEFIANT DISORDER IN FOREST SCHOOL

- This is another case where resistance to adult control is at the forefront of the behaviours. Your status with other children does not matter much. Your standing with this child is what counts. It's also another case where a learner might do as you say because it's you, not because it's a rule. So, strive to develop that relationship. As with CD, you might again approach it with a certain coolness at first, avoiding being overly joyous, as ODD children can respond to this in a negative way. I'll also adopt similar praise strategies to those used with CD, for example triangulated praise. Instructions are better phrased as, 'It's raining; what do we need to do before we leave the shelter?', rather than, 'Right, get your waterproofs on!'

- ODD children will frequently struggle to establish long-term positive friendships. Other children often choose to ignore them, leading to isolation, loneliness and behaviour reactive to this such as attention seeking and verbal abuse towards peers. The forest school environment might itself offer new opportunities to build better peer relationships, and you can enhance these opportunities. Clever use of praise, including the ODD learner in activities in a pivotal way, catching them being (socially) good, and of course, having the positive bias that shows your focus is on what goes right, not wrong are all useful strategies. Also consider how you might model the behaviour that you want to see from others. Getting emotional when something does not go according to plan should not be evident in your behaviour.

- These children can frequently go into crisis. This gives us many opportunities to support them to learn how to raise the bar in terms of their ability to cope. Post-crisis, aim to have the ABC conversation. This looks at the Antecedents to, Behaviour during, and Consequences after, an incident. So, you will talk calmly about what led to the behaviour, (briefly) what the problem behaviour was, and then the consequences for the child and others. This should include the sanctions resulting from the incident as well as the feelings that were caused by it. This isn't meant to be a guilt trip for the child, so keep it free of that tone. They just need to see the cause and effect structure here. You will also want to explore coping strategies for next time. Crucially though, you should look to do this when they have made great behaviour choices too; you are connecting pathways in the brain and introducing a new way of thinking.

- If you yourself have a huge personality, perhaps a reactive one, managing ODD children can be a tricky challenge. Don't rise to the bait, don't engage in debate and don't take it personally! If you find this happening, use this technique: imagine their parent on your shoulder. Think about what you're about to say to the child. If you feel you'd still say it if their parent was present, then go ahead. If you wouldn't, find a different way to respond. Another way to judge it is to consider a professional speaking to your own child in the way you're about to speak to this ODD learner, and if it seems wrong, then stop talking!

- ODD learners, especially older ones, can do a lot of tutting, posturing, raising eyebrows, rolling their eyes and so on! As long as they are still compliant, I use a technique called tactical ignoring. I rarely challenge secondary behaviours like this if they are complaining while being compliant (i.e., moaning about having to do something, but doing it at the same time). Of course, in some cases, it is not beneficial to fail to respond, and you will know when this is the case, but typically it is when children need to see a response for the greater good, rather than because you are personally offended. There might also be times when I will choose to follow an incident up at a later time, perhaps at the end of the day, or some other time when I can see that the child is in a more reflective mood.

- As with some other earlier conditions, issuing a choice script, coupled with the walkaway technique – moving away and engaging with another learner – can be effective. Because I like employing a positive bias, I'll seek also to remind them of when they were brilliant (fingers crossed there's been such an event...) and even smile as I turn away. This is high-status behaviour from you, remember; you fully expect them to make a better choice. So, it might go something like, 'Peter, you can join us for the nature walk, or you can carry on with this behaviour, in which case you will miss it. I'd love you to make the better choice; you knew lots about the birds we saw last time. Make that choice, thanks.' Follow this with a smile, and then turn to chat with the group.

- Low resilience can be an issue with ODD. Forest school is inherently wonderful as a tonic to this, as discussed elsewhere in this book, but you will need to present any specific activities you want to do carefully. I like to introduce activities that almost everyone will fail at in the first instance, if not many times! Equally, children might set themselves real challenges. I know, of course, that small, achievable tasks are part of forest school, where children can experience success, build in confidence and so on. I'm just saying that we shouldn't be scared of the less achievable, because amazing learning opportunities exist there. Success is not my primary concern; I'm interested in effort. In the past, I've even said, 'If I was marking this out of ten, I'd give you one point for success but the other nine for effort.' In theory then, someone who finds it easy, or is successful through luck, might get one mark; someone who tries and tries but is ultimately unsuccessful, would get nine! Group activities that mean learners fail on a team level (and laugh about it) can be brilliant too; it's easier to fail in a group, right? A great example would be the Group Bow Drill Challenge, which requires, say, five people at one end of a rope, five at the other, with the rope wrapped around the bow drill, and another two learners holding the bearing block. By pulling back and forth, the team generate smoke and heat and hopefully an ember under the drill, which can be ignited with a tinder bundle. Almost everybody fails at this the first time (I did once have a group of outdoor education students who got it first time, which was amazing). Gently exposing a child with low resilience to the concept that failing is okay, and actually that failing might be sometimes our first step to success, is a good thing. Forest school offers lots of opportunities to boost resilience, which I discuss elsewhere in the book.

- ODD learners can rarely wait for a reward they've earned! Keep rewards simple but tangible. They can be a high five, a smile, round of applause; it doesn't have to be an all-expenses trip to Santorini or a sports car... Praise must be genuine, though; anything other will be noticed by the child and potentially cause an adverse reaction.

- Low self-esteem can be improved wonderfully through team games, again mentioned elsewhere in this book. I do like to have planned activities of this type. I recognize that just being in a forest school where the learning is entirely child led can be a perfect environment for exposure to all the benefits we want for children, just inherent in the interactions with peers, adults and nature. But I think we can nudge things in the right direction for complex cases too. The best of both worlds!

- Structure and routines from the start help to create a sense of both safety and certainty. Establish these from, not day one, but minute one. You can often reduce the likelihood of behaviour issues in this way, like a true behaviour ninja. Remember with ODD, rules (and routines) are easier to swallow (and follow) when peers are doing the same...

Autism spectrum disorder (ASD)

There is already a great guide to working with ASD in forest school, so I won't attempt to reinvent the wheel here,[1] but rather suggest some behavioural gems. My experience with ASD has been wide and varied (it is a spectrum, after all). I've worked with autistic learners in specialist provisions, including those where autism has been the primary diagnosis, but where behaviour support has been the primary focus. I've worked with autism through the home-educated community, and

---

1   James, M. (2018). *Forest School and Autism: A Practical Guide*. London: Jessica Kingsley Publishers.

with sensory support groups. I will draw on this experience in my comments here.

I still meet (professional) people who tell me a child 'can't' be on the autism spectrum because he 'told me a joke/gave me eye contact/ was very sociable'. Remember you are dealing with a spectrum here – a range of possible traits and much variation in how these will present, or indeed, are masked. So autistic learners' interactions with you will depend on where they are on the spectrum, and to what extent they utilize learned masking techniques. While in many cases I might avoid such statements as 'He laughed his head off', in response to which some ASD learners might quite genuinely want to know exactly how it was reattached, I have met others who will understand such phrases. I've had conversations rich in humour, irony and subtlety. So for me, working with these learners requires us to tap into any additional adult support that comes with them, and learn quickly. I would also say I have found ASD learners to be a delight to work with at forest school. As with all challenging cases, of course, there will always be a need to deal with complexities, and our positivity will help. I'm not overly focused on what the learners who attend forest school cannot do; rather, I'm thinking about working with their strengths and seeing where that takes us.

MANAGING AUTISM SPECTRUM DISORDER IN FOREST SCHOOL

- Structures and routines will be part of your approach, as we have discussed. They will be part of how you deliver forest school – tool talks, safety around the fire, boundaries – but also, part of your approach to behaviour. These will be of benefit to ASD learners. The predictability and certainty of these things form the stable base from which these learners can explore, without, as one ASD boy told me, 'getting my boxes all jumbled'. In fact, the routines, methodical skills and consistent elements of forest school can help ASD learners to thrive in the outdoor environment.

- As far as social skills go, I exercise caution here. It's too easy, for example, to see an ASD child sitting apart from other learners and look at this from your own perspective. You might feel 'sorry' for the child, and encourage them to join in. The problem I've found with this is that my discomfort with the situation, my desire to change it, is unimportant. How does the child feel? Some might be entirely comfortable with the situation; in fact, it might be desirable to them to have things remain as they are. Then along comes well-meaning me, injecting some stress into their day, forcing interactions on them! This being said, I want the same outcomes for my ASD learners as I do for all; I'd like them to be equipped with the skills to be able to manage the world around them in the future. So I do try to introduce the opportunities to develop social skills further, but I don't force participation. I'll often focus on co-operative skills such as turn taking, shared problem solving, negotiation and taking a variety of roles within a group. And of course, I know that children occupying themselves with tasks they have chosen themselves is common and positive and a great learning opportunity in forest school.

- I like all my learners, early on in their forest school experience, to have their own sit spot. This has benefits in many ways and is a concept most forest school leaders will know and understand. For ASD learners, this spot can be useful as a place where they can be calm if their boxes do get 'jumbled'. Sensory overload can be a problem for ASD learners, but so can sensory-seeking behaviour. So that feeling you get when fingernails are dragged down a blackboard (remember those?) can be triggered for ASD learners by what we might consider typical sensory experiences. Equally, an ASD child performing a rocking motion can suggest that additional sensory input is being sought, often helping to redress some imbalance they feel, or enable them to self-regulate in some other way. Therefore, encourage ASD learners to use their sit spot whenever they need to. Other self-regulatory techniques might be in evidence and these are fine too. One learner who attends one of our forest schools needs some time to skip throughout his day with us, and will now just let me know he's 'off for a skip'. We remind him of the limits of range, and away he goes. He'll often select to do this when he knows we are preparing a change of activity.

- I like to give a little warning of activity change. I might let learners know my thoughts on activities or key moments like lunch, from early in the day. I'll give a ten-, five- and one-minute warning of change too. Of course, I do want to be able to equip ASD learners with the skills that go with the unpredictability that is part of the child-led approach to forest school. I'll usually cover this in our first meeting and reinforce it periodically, with a 'routine' for coping with that lack of routine! This can include an opt-out option too. It will begin something like this: 'Sometimes we will just suddenly decide to do something unexpected; that's okay as it's good to respond to opportunities nature gives us. But you don't have to. Instead you can...'

- Of course, consistency can be that stabilizer that some ASD learners need, so I strive to have consistency of approach at all times and, from a behaviour point of view, to be consistently patient and kind. I want all my learners to know that 'When I do A, Dave will respond with B', and I want this certainty to mean safety for them. Don't find yourself introducing a routine or approach, with the best of intentions, only to find yourself three sessions later not bothering with it. This is tough for ASD children and tells all learners that you are inconsistent – a low-status behaviour that we want to avoid at all costs. And note that spontaneity is not the same as inconsistency.

Pathological demand avoidance (PDA)

Related to ASD, this syndrome manifests generally as an almost obsessive tendency to resist or avoid control by adults. This seems to stem from an anxiety about, and drive to be in, control. PDA is quite a challenge even for an experienced behaviour manager, as often our usual behaviour approaches just don't work. What a wonderful opportunity to develop new ones, then!

Much of my experience with PDA in forest school has been with home-educated children. I'm not sure if this reflects the number of children who struggle so much with this condition in the school setting that parents frequently remove them, or if there are other factors at play. I have worked with a number of diagnosed PDA children and young people, and possibly more who are undiagnosed or misdiagnosed (often with ODD, ADHD, or personality disorder). In all cases, I have learned a lot from conversations with parents and carers, and I recommend this route to you. They will have learned lots of ways to navigate this potential maze.

Perhaps nowhere else is the importance of perspective better illustrated than here! In my opinion, it is vital to enter into this working relationship with a positive, lively and enquiring mind. Don't think of this as a power struggle you must win at all costs; instead, view it as an opportunity for learning. The skills developed in managing PDA, in class or in forest school, will improve your success rate with many other challenging learners. So, embrace the opportunity! For example, how you phrase instructions in order to get buy-in from a PDA learner will work with oppositional children, some conduct disordered children, and those who just seem to be having a belligerent moment (especially younger children). Also, in a lesson on the value of being proactive in managing behaviour, there is no better teacher than the learner with PDA, as we shall see.

MANAGING PATHOLOGICAL DEMAND AVOIDANCE
IN FOREST SCHOOL

- When learners are displaying a high level of demand avoidant behaviour, this will often have high anxiety at its root and therefore should be managed with this in mind. This is not the time to take things personally. For that reason, structures and routines, explained, taught and embedded from the start, really are very important. But...PDA learners don't usually respond to them when this is done in the usual way. So, we might decide that we develop our routines with a more indirect style, incorporating a little negotiation. Rather than simply stating, for example, routines for starting the day (arriving at the fire circle, where bags go, tending the fire and so on), a more effective route might include questions that invite useful solutions, such as, 'You know, I'm concerned people might trip over bags if we just dump them anywhere. Do you have any ideas about how we might manage that?' Another option which I have used successfully with PDA/ASD and demand avoidant children has been to capitalize on the fact that sometimes they will accept the rules of a 'higher authority'. So, if I say, 'This is a Health and Safety rule; there's no room to change it. It's just how it has to be', I can often get compliance. This is where most of my non-negotiables lie, of course, and it is vital to have a small number of these.

- Collaboration, negotiation and respect go a long way to build trusting and effective working relationships with PDA children. I will usually look for win–win solutions. It is vital that we always remain calm, never bear a grudge and aim for change in the long term, not just winning individual battles.

- Flexibility is useful, and forest school can lend itself to this very effectively. The very essence of a child-led approach can play to the positives of PDA children – their intelligence, creativity and determination, for example. Don't miss these opportunities.

- Remember how we use scripts for predictable issues? You may find yourself needing that 'get out' script for times when a demand avoidant child is really digging their heels in, as this will often be accompanied by rising anxiety and a risk of overload. It might include a reference to their sit spot: 'I think we've gone as far as we can go with this; I'm going to step away, you can use your sit spot, of course; it's your choice.'

- Rephrasing of instructions will, as with our approach to routines, reduce any perception of demand, and remember, a PDA child is hypersensitive to the possibility that you are attempting to control them. 'I wonder how we could...' is good, as is 'Let's see if...' I recall a PDA learner who was very light skinned and very sensitive to sunlight, in a group I had on a guided walk. As we stopped for lunch, his carer put some sunblock on a tree stump next to him, simply said, 'There's some sunblock', and moved away – no demands, no, 'You need...', 'You must...' (it worked!).

- Indirect communication works too. I might hand a pair of safety gloves to a child who's about to use a saw, while speaking to another. I could, if a number of learners including the PDA child are doing the same activity, give instructions to the mass rather than the individual. I might introduce a competitive or game element to an activity: 'Let's see who can collect the most different leaves off the forest floor.'

- Choice scripts, accompanied by the walkaway technique, can be useful, but ensure that your body language, facial expression and tone do not communicate demand, control or impending doom!

- I steer clear of most individual rewards, especially those that are accompanied by a 'do this and you'll get that' situation, because to a PDA or other power-sensitive child, the sense of control being applied is absolute. 'You need to do it *and* I control the reward too' is what they hear. Far better are spontaneous, high-value/low-cost rewards such as a smile, a thumbs-up and sincere verbal praise. I recommend, of course, that you are thoughtful about verbal praise. I've seen PDA (and other) children destroy their own work when they have been praised for it. Try to de-personalize the praise and shift the focus from the child and the work they've done, to what you think of it: 'You've done a great job of carving that spoon' or, 'That is a fantastic spoon you've made' can result in 'No I haven't' or 'No it's not, it's rubbish!' More subtle would be, 'I'd be happy to use such a spoon' or, 'That spoon has just the right shape.'

- I'm cautious with sanctions too. This is just more power being applied. I'm not saying don't use them, just use them with that heightened level of awareness. It is often enough of a sanction to withdraw attention; I don't need to find myself furiously whittling in a corner somewhere, grumbling to myself about how 'in my day...' One of the wonderful things about learning in nature is that there is feedback from the environment – it is inherent in that environment and completely neutral and this can work wonders. I don't mean that you should let a child choose not to use a tool safely, so that they can learn from the resultant injury! But if your PDA child is feeling a little colder than they need to, because they refused to put a hat on, well... nature won't raise the temperature, will it? If you decide to run through the brambles when instructed otherwise, your clothes will get snagged, maybe torn. You can shout about it, complain, melt down, even. But guess what happens next time you run through the brambles? Yes, the child has met the immovable object; a learning experience and an opportunity for you to (gently) use that ABC of behaviour technique.

- Forest school often has a good ratio of adults to children, so use this to your advantage if you find yourself in this lucky position. If you can have a PDA child supported one to one by an adult who is aware of the condition and the strategies to adopt, then this can work wonders. Equally, if you are supported by an adult who does not subscribe to the idea of being a calm, professional and positive member of a team, give them the job of maintaining the fire and limit their contact with your PDA learners!

- Participation in team activities and being able to take a range of different roles within a team are desirable targets to aim for in the long term with PDA learners. So when children or young people have decided on an activity, take the opportunity to influence choices of role or facilitate a discussion about this, so that everybody who wants to can be a leader or whatever. This is a good experience for a PDA child.

- Learn to anticipate avoidant behaviour, including distraction techniques, making excuses and hiding. Have plans, scripts and solutions prepared. The setting and embedding of physical boundaries is a good example, with the 'higher power' of Health and Safety being the reason, of course.

Social, emotional and mental health (SEMH) issues

When a child has unmet social, emotional or mental health needs, they can communicate this in many and varied ways that are inappropriate in comparison with 'typical' responses. This can include such a range of behaviours as verbal and physical aggression, anger, frustration, self-harm and complex manipulative behaviour, to name but a few. Left without intervention, this can develop into high-risk behaviours, including criminal acts.

Having worked for over a quarter of a century with SEMH learners, I can tell you that relationships are crucial. But unfortunately, we can't expect them to be a cure-all or a 'dead cert'. Equally, firm, fair and clear boundaries matter but are not a guarantee. It has taken years for the child with SEMH issues to develop into the complex young person, causing havoc in educational settings, including your forest school; you shouldn't expect to play anything other than the long game with some of these youngsters. I can remember regular discussions with brilliant colleagues about being 'consistently flexible' or 'flexibly consistent'! The inexperienced would roll their eyes at the never-ending debate, but the wiser heads would think about it – do they amount to the same thing or are they opposites? I still don't know, but being a reflective practitioner is vital when dealing with SEMH, more so I would wager than almost any other area of SEND.

SEMH children will often carry multiple labels and diagnoses, including CD, ODD, ADHD, attachment disorder, PTSD, the list goes on. In my experience, these young people can delight and surprise you as often as they can make you feel despair and frustration. And for all that, I'd recommend working with these learners to anyone. I've worked with primary and secondary age SEMH children and I feel these complex individuals need the best teachers and the best professionals around them. They need our patience and understanding more than almost any other complex cases, and will test these qualities in us more than we thought possible.

Although many educators might shudder at the prospect of taking SEMH learners outdoors, reaching for their pens and blank risk assessments with trembling fingers, I think outdoor learning, including forest school, should be a staple of their educational diet, written into every SEMH education, health and care plan (EHCP) before the child's name is added to the top. It is crucial to remember that many of the difficulties and challenges associated with SEMH do not have to be for life. With the right interventions, care and support, children with these issues can overcome them and go on to live healthy, successful lives.

MANAGING SOCIAL, EMOTIONAL AND MENTAL HEALTH ISSUES IN FOREST SCHOOL

- We need to familiarize ourselves with all the strategies mentioned for any conditions where there is co-morbidity because those techniques may be relevant. This is why building a positive relationship, quickly and carefully, is paramount. Without doubt, these learners are capable of defying all rules, but following you because you are important to them. They could realistically be the scourge of a local community, but make much better choices when they are with you. As a starting point, consider the techniques we discussed for ODD.

- Actively coach social skills. Model good social interaction, how to cope in difficult situations, how you cope with stress. Include team activities (and take advantage of those that naturally and frequently occur in forest school) that gently expose them to developing and earning trust, building communication skills, and playing varied roles in the group. I have listed some examples in Chapter 8, 'Opportunities and Activities to Support Behaviour Change'.

- Ensure you teach behaviour, almost as if it was a curriculum in its own right. Again, you can model this. If you shout and get angry when you have run out of coping mechanisms, why would you expect learners to be any different?

- You will need to work diligently on presenting yourself as a high-status person. Remember that this status goes hand in hand with calm, relaxed behaviour. Dithering, uncertain, flummoxed behaviour is not going to help. In cases like this, the learner becomes the lion, and you are the limping gazelle! Use strategies that help us to remain calm (or at least, to 'fake it until we make it'). This includes prepared scripts – focus on choice scripts and your 'get out' script. Delivering these with the right pace, pitch, tone and volume will be vital too.

- The best long-term strategy I use with SEMH issues is the positive bias approach. I aim to give good behaviour choices my attention and praise, but this must be meaningful; they will resent any signs of superficiality in praise, and are expert at detecting it. Reinforce and reward good behaviour choices!

- Play to their strengths. You need to get to know your SEMH learners first, of course, but many are leaders within a group. This can often manifest itself as a negative because they can become the ringleaders of poor behaviour. But because of your perspective, you will see a good attribute being used in a poor way, and work to nudge things a little. Give them responsibility, respect their opinions, consider their views and you will get a return on the investment.

- Repair and reconnect following any problems or occasions where you have needed to address poor behaviour choices. Remember, the problem is the problem, not the child.

- Low resilience can be a factor, well hidden though it may be, especially in older learners. Fortunately, there are many, many forest school and bushcraft activities that develop and nurture resilience in a non-threatening way and I have included a number of them in Chapter 8 on practical activities.

- If I do need to use sanctions, they've been explained in advance to the group, and I inch my way through them, while being consistent in their use. I use them predictably because what I want is for a learner to see where a situation is heading, and make a conscious decision to change that. I want them to develop a new habit of making better behaviour choices. My sanctions vary according to age and SEND, but as an example, for secondary age SEMH, I raise their awareness that there is a problem: 'John, can you complete the task I set? Thanks.' I'll issue a first warning, then a final warning (and please note there's only one of these), then there will be a consequence such as removal for a period, loss of access to an activity, or whatever I have set out as a motivation. During this, I am doing everything I can to avoid the next 'rung' on the ladder. For example, if I've raised their awareness, by telling the learner what they need to do (rather than 'Stop doing...' the other thing), and then the behaviour carries on, I might ask the question, 'Do you need my help with that?', which really means, 'You're still not behaving in an acceptable way.' Then I give the first warning. Still not making better choices? Then it might be, 'John, just pop over here and show me your progress with that carving.' This gives me (and John) another chance. Then if necessary comes the final warning, at which point I've helped all I can, and I'll be sure to make that clear when we have our ABC conversation later. This will raise the bar for next time.

- Make sure your perspective is right with SEMH; a clean slate next day is important for any child, but for the SEMH learner, a clean slate might be required more often! You must take on the three mantras and live them; nowhere will your determination be more tested than with SEMH, but that makes your successes all the sweeter.

Post-traumatic stress disorder (PTSD)

PTSD and other adverse childhood experiences (ACE) are complex and deeply saddening and require the best of us in terms of compassion and, at times, patience. Reactive behaviour can be very challenging.

PTSD is an anxiety disorder that has perhaps come more to the fore in recent decades as a condition suffered by many armed forces personnel following traumatic events in conflicts. Other causes are many and varied and can include serious road traffic accidents, violent assaults and the sudden death of significant people in a person's life. I have worked with many young people diagnosed with this condition and they can present with a range of behaviours from fearful to aggressive.

There are many treatments available, including medication and various therapies. Time for relaxation in a natural environment is effective, and clearly forest school can provide this. There are examples of the woodland environment being used for therapy and relaxation across the world, and many military veterans benefit from such opportunities, including courses run by me and my colleagues.

If you are working with young people who have PTSD, it makes sense to get as much information as you can, perhaps through parents or carers if that is appropriate, or the school, social workers and perhaps medical professionals if that is possible. You need to be aware of any therapies currently under way, what triggers there might be, and how the PTSD might manifest in the individual. Educational psychologists can be invaluable here. The PTSD learner may, for example, be accessing play therapy, and it is useful for you to be aware of this.

Young people with PTSD might present with a range of behaviours during forest school, including acting out, disruptive actions, rudeness towards adults, low concentration, unpredictability (seemingly odd or bizarre behaviour), low confidence and self-esteem, and hypersensitivity. Some of these reactions can be driven by a simple trigger, for example an adult raising their voice, causing a fight/flight/freeze response. On a positive note, however, any forest school leader can probably recognize many aspects of the environment in which we work that can help. Let's look at this:

- Nature is a healer in its own right; it takes no effort to find research conclusions that show this. Being in green spaces is good for us all. Time to observe, contemplate and just 'be' in nature can benefit those with PTSD.

- Our predictable routines will offer the stability, reliability and certainty that will help those with PTSD to cope. This is because we've introduced them for exactly that reason – there should be no great surprises here for the young person: 'I know that if I do A, B will happen.' This in itself creates security.

- It usually takes very little time for the learner to see the woods as a non-threatening place, even die-hard city types. Accelerate this process with regular 'walk and talk' early in their forest school experience, where you explain what is going on and you read the 'news of the woods': who left that track, what this tree is called, which animal made that noise.

MANAGING POST-TRAUMATIC STRESS DISORDER IN FOREST SCHOOL

- Build relaxation into the day. Again, our wondrous sit spots can be a great help here and I would always encourage the use of these, but I have also used guided meditation in a very simple format with these learners and have found it of benefit.

- If you can involve their 'key adults' in forest school, so much the better. Even a chance to pop in at the end of a term can help the child, as they connect with that important person in a new environment, demonstrate their new skills, and show some pride in what they have achieved. Having purpose can be important.

- Give them plenty of opportunities to experience some joy! In fact, that goes for everyone, but watching wildlife 'do its thing' is joyful. We have a kingfisher on the river on one of our sites and seeing that flash of blue is without doubt a joyful event for our learners. So too is listening to a woodpecker drumming on a spring morning, or seeing a glimpse of a roe deer... We can manufacture these opportunities too with wildlife surveys, from the biggest to the smallest creatures. It helps if you can give some learners with PTSD a specific role in this task – again, the purpose is beneficial here. But keep this subtle if you feel the learner is lacking in resilience, or is perhaps avoidant.

- It's important that you do not take any behaviour that's directed at you personally. Equally, try to remain non-judgemental when the learner displays what can be extreme behaviours. Remember this is all anxiety driven and the purpose of the behaviour is often avoidant: 'How can I get out of this situation that's causing me (or might cause me) to revisit traumatic events?' With PTSD, children can seem to need 'time out' when in fact 'time in' (time with an understanding and skilled adult) is more preferable. Talking to a PTSD child calmly when they are struggling, particularly younger children, means you can co-regulate the behaviour before expecting the child to self-regulate. Model the approach you want them to adopt, and be aware of your body language and tone of voice to a minute degree at this point. Remember, they might be hypervigilant and so see threat where there is none.

- Negative self-image and thinking are common. We will cover activities that will help to address this in Chapter 8 on practical activities but remember that small successes need to be noticed for many learners with PTSD. Progress can move at glacial speed and positives can be tiny, but if you don't notice them, what is the point? Refusal to participate is usually driven by fear of failure, or perhaps of peer interactions. To avoid the refusal, notice the little victories from the start. Also, make the bigger activities a 'challenge by choice', which they can opt into, or just observe. Notice if they manage to contribute from the sidelines – you'll eventually get them involved!

Remember, and this is key, overcoming PTSD can take time. I've seen short-term PTSD in response to loss significantly hamper and impact a child's behaviour for six months, but often it is far, far longer.

Attachment disorder (AD)

It is a sad truth that many children have missed the opportunity, as an infant, to form a secure attachment with a main caregiver. This can result from neglect, abuse, substance misuse, carer imprisonment, but also post-natal depression, carer absence due to their job, serious illness and more. I say this to illustrate that there is no point in judging parents or carers at this point, and certainly no need for assumptions. I do recognize, of course, that many readers may have worked with families where a whole sibling group has been left with attachment issues, where social services are heavily involved, causes are well documented, and so on. In those cases, we all hope the relevant support has been put in place while you work your magic in forest school!

Attachment disorder can present in a number of specific forms so it is worth doing some research. That is beyond the scope of this book, however; we will instead look at a range of possible behaviours and how we can effectively support the learner to make better choices. And what a range! You could get anything from damage to property, disruptive, manipulative and attention-seeking behaviour, to overly 'clingy' withdrawn and tearful behaviour.

Imagine being a child, arriving at your forest school with a sense that you are not to be trusted, that you are not a 'safe' person. It's an appalling thought, I know, but it guides us to the perspective we need if we want to develop that effective working relationship I keep mentioning. With that relationship in place, you can begin to show these learners, whatever their age, that you can support them to make better behaviour choices.

MANAGING ATTACHMENT DISORDER IN FOREST SCHOOL

- The use of rewards and sanctions is a common and often effective strategy in schools. It supports the overwhelming majority of young people to choose well with their behaviour. At a basic level, it works by rewarding 'good', desirable behaviour and sanctioning 'bad', unwanted behaviour. I feel that sometimes we do children a disservice if we don't use this approach. I have genuinely experienced children taking advantage of a rewards-only system, perceiving the adult as weak, rather than kind. As a default setting, I recommend it and if you work in a school, you'll understand your school's own system. If you are an outside provider, it might be that behaviour continues to be managed by attending staff using their system. You should feel free to use it. But also know when not to. Some children and young people cannot help making a poor behaviour choice in some situations. This might be because they are poorly equipped by their previous experiences with the necessary social skills to manage, or they are anxious, or they have attention issues, or... With AD, this is definitely a case of the problem being the problem, not the child. I will talk very carefully with a child with attachment issues and try to get to the bottom of what drove the behaviour. And you'll know, of course, that, like any number of the complex cases we discuss here, anxiety may play a large part in it. So separate the behaviour from the child, keep a lively, positive, problem-solving approach and do what's needed to equip the learner to make better choices next time, or maybe the time after – rarely will we find quick fixes here. Also, I much prefer to praise effort rather than success with many learners, so with a rewards system I am rewarding the level of effort, not the fact that they were successful. Therefore, a child who has really tried hard all day to make the best behaviour choices, and then ultimately finishes that day on a poor choice, still needs my positive comments.

- Routines! What, again? Yes, you're getting the message – routines are the foundation of a life-changing classroom or forest school. Remember, routines can create security and certainty and communicate your high expectations of everyone.

- I sometimes find that, even in forest school, a seating plan of sorts can help anxious children. I might sit a nervous child with attachment issues near me and near the 'exit' of the fire area, so that I can monitor things and they can leave if they need to without being overly 'noticeable' to others. I also allow a buddy to sit next to them, someone who is helpful and supportive. It is a shame to see so many attachment disordered learners moved away from friends as a consequence of their behaviour, at which point it often escalates. I am not worried about dealing with an escalation (I've done a course...) but I don't see the need for one in most situations.

- Explaining the plan for the day can be beneficial to AD learners as much as it can to those with ASD. The structure is good for them. However, I'll always include a mention of when nature 'gives us an opportunity', and let them know that a change of plan is okay and can lead to something exciting.

- Attention-seeking behaviour is common with AD and can sometimes be quite bizarre. With any attention seeker, regardless of SEND or complex needs, I usually find that giving unsolicited attention (i.e., attention they didn't actively seek) is effective. I love this technique and use it with loud, 'in your face' Year 11 girls as frequently as I do with primary spotlight stealers! It tells them, 'I'll give you attention; that's what I'm here for. No need to climb 20 feet above the forest floor.' Giving such learners tasks to do can also be beneficial. By building their independence in this way, they still have that connection with you, they know they are 'on your radar', because you delegated a task to them, and there is no need to seek your attention more forcefully, shall we say!

- Quiet time is good for most AD learners. Those sit spots will be well worn by now! Guided meditation and mindfulness sessions are also good.

- Risk-taking behaviour, perhaps as part of attention seeking, can be common, so be really clear with tool talks, monitor learners closely and make use of additional adults, preferably those who have a connection with the child.

- I use those complex approaches to praise, such as triangulated praise, when I am developing my relationship with AD learners, especially older ones. I also use instruct/walkaway, anticipate compliance, and other assertive techniques. My high status needs to be clear with these learners, but I do it cautiously; I'm not in a power struggle here.

- With AD, you'll get some of the resistance to adult control that we've talked about with PDA, CD, ODD and others. This will manifest differently with each learner, so familiarize yourself with all of the techniques for managing this!

- De-escalation strategies may become necessary despite your best efforts. Don't worry about this. Stay calm and think about everything you say. Give the tone of voice you use, your body language and facial expression acute attention. If you get argumentative behaviour from the young person, you can manage this with scripts and frameworks to guide what you say. One example I use with such learners is the acknowledge/apologize/ agree frame. Let's say I have an AD child who is verbally confrontational: 'It's not fair! I want to try the archery. You said I could this morning!' Using the frame, my response might be something like, 'I can see that you are upset about that (acknowledge); I am sorry you feel that way (apologize); I can understand how that might make you feel frustrated (agree). Now, we need to find a solution...' You will note that I can do an apology even if I feel I don't have anything to apologize for, and I can agree with their feelings if nothing else! What this does is show some willingness to see their perspective, give me time to think and them time to calm a little, so that we can find an outcome (which might well not include archery...).

- Remember that you might also need your 'get out' script prepared...

Some of the most upsetting cases I have worked with have been children with attachment issues. It can be heartbreaking but remember that you will need to put those emotions to one side and deal with the challenges with compassion and understanding. There are rarely any quick fixes, but you can support these learners to find a way out of their difficulties, and it is rewarding to do so.

Low resilience

As a complexity, low resilience might seem fairly minor until you meet children who have developed all manner of poor behaviour habits as a result! That's when you'll find yourself reaching for this book and thumbing through it with trembling fingers. The child who has a low resilience threshold and is attending your forest school is, however, very fortunate indeed. You are going to work wonders with and for them. Forest school is a nurturing environment; it's an outdoor experience that will provide all the inherent feedback that a learner with low resilience needs to overcome this issue, to improve their resilience and raise their 'coping bar' higher and higher.

I have 'prescribed' forest school for children who can't cope, for example, with getting maths problems wrong. Exercise books and pens go flying across the room, foreheads are resolutely attached to the desk top, tears flow... This is one of the amazing things about using forest school as a problem-solver. An issue in class can be addressed outdoors and the child returns to class better equipped emotionally, socially and behaviourally, whatever the original problem was.

Resilience is the ability to cope with the knocks we get in life. Children with low resilience will perceive many events as 'knocks' when perhaps their more resilient peers would hardly consider it. I've seen children go into emotional meltdown when their pencil tip snaps; others reach for the sharpener and get on with their day. Now, you might have a 'get a grip', 'man up' kind of script in your head (I understand this), but please leave it there! It's not typically going to help the situation, nor is it the approach of a professional educator, unless you arrived here via time travel from a school in the 1970s.

Low resilience can sit alongside many conditions as part of them or as an added complexity, while not being a condition in its own right. For example, learners with PTSD typically have a lower tolerance for setbacks and often avoid situations where they are likely to fail.

MANAGING LOW RESILIENCE IN FOREST SCHOOL

- Be positive! Have a bright and cheerful outlook when problems occur. They are not dead ends, they are obstacles for us to overcome, happenings that improve us as people and therefore things to look forward to. Model this specifically as those learners with low resilience need to be taught the skills and the perspective. Explore stories of resilience in the great outdoors; there are thousands of them. Teach a simple framework for a task so that, if the framework is followed, success is more likely.

If unsuccessful, revisit the framework with that same lively, enquiring mind, and work out the next step. Although we normally focus on effort and not the final outcome, in this case we will be flexible because this is about introducing a new way of thinking for the child. But see below.

- Effort, not success, in other situations, will be the usual way you go. Focus on their strengths but remember that we need to focus also on the smallest signs of improvement here. Lots of the skills forest school learners need to develop are new to them all, of course, and this is useful to us because 'failure' will be normal. We should normalize failing. See it as a step towards success and make sure the learners do too. I have a script here: 'No worries. Getting it wrong is often the first step to getting it right.' I use it a lot in forest school!

- I might also use a technique called language for security. This is where I anticipate and legitimize failure. For example, 'Okay, we're going to try an activity now, and when I tested it on my own children, it took them four attempts before they succeeded. I was really impressed because I thought it might take more...' Failure is normalized in one statement, making it more palatable to the learner with low resilience (and others).

- If a learner with low resilience is displaying negative behaviour, perhaps it is driven by a need to avoid an activity. Can you give them an alternative role? I'm not saying back down from every instruction, just that you should be prepared to play the long game, and, of course, to think on your feet if a real meltdown looks imminent.

- Younger children can benefit from distraction techniques if they are struggling. When you see that anxiety developing, can you intervene, perhaps ask them for their help with something else?

- Of course, being a proactive person means you can plan for using the techniques above; if you know genuinely that a task might be beyond their ability to cope, try altering it to support them, without making it obvious. Can they work in a team? Can they play a part role, avoiding the 'hardest' part, but still getting the gentle challenge they require? I might do this with the Group Bow Drill Challenge. Their role could be the least taxing, perhaps holding the bearing block (this activity is explained later).

- I have said we need to teach behaviour. I often have a focus on developing resilience – it could be a whole day of challenge, or less if appropriate, with a range of tasks and activities for this purpose. I use a mantra with younger children: 'Never give in, you'll eventually win.' It's wonderful to hear one child use this mantra when advising another child who is struggling. See Chapter 8 for more on activities that raise resilience.

While I see more and more evidence that teachers are worried about a lack of resilience in young people today, and I deliver training regularly on how to manage it in the classroom, I know that forest school can be a huge part of the solution. With careful management, we can support learners to step out of these difficulties. They can develop new skills that will have benefits across the range of their learning in school and beyond. It's not too gooey to say that forest school can change the lives of children with low resilience.

Chapter 8

OPPORTUNITIES AND ACTIVITIES TO SUPPORT BEHAVIOUR CHANGE

A statement before we start, before I'm accused of not understanding forest school, diluting the purity of the approach, undermining the ethos, and so on! First, I am a level 3 forest school leader. I've done the course. I get the underlying tenets. I know there are forest school leaders who profess to run sessions with no planned activities, literally working as a facilitator and guide. These leaders have lots of equipment and no plan, so that, whatever the children come up with, they can run with it. Guess what? I do this too. So do the team I work with and for. Those days might be my favourite kind; they certainly are common occurrences in our forest schools. I also recognize that, in some cases, that approach can help children with complex needs, those who display challenging behaviour and SEND learners too, with no adaptation.

But I don't, for the sake of this, need to 'keep the faith' or miss out on opportunities. Neither do I value this purity over a child's right to experience what the woods have to offer. In that situation, preferences about forest school models will come a poor second. And in fact, a school in England not making adequate provision for SEND children to be able to access the offer at that school could and should find itself in a lot of trouble. It is expected that a school will make such adjustments as are necessary and reasonable to ensure that access. I must confess to some frustration when a well-meaning but newly qualified forest school leader asks for some ideas for activities, only to be bombarded with comments such as, 'If you plan it, it's not forest school' or, 'Well, not strictly forest school, but...' I prefer just to give them some suggestions. I can't know the detail of their situation every time. I can't know their context. I'm just going to presume that they're setting out with the wish to do well by the children they work with, perhaps aiming to address some issues and do some good. They're not, in my opinion, aiming to bring the forest school movement to its knees from within.

Finally, my belief that we can use forest school, with adaptations, to help all children to overcome difficulties is paramount. I don't want children to miss out. I want to adapt so that they can experience what forest school offers their peers. If a few planned and co-ordinated activities find their way into my otherwise learner-led forest school, that's fine with me. So, in the following pages you will find stand-alone activities which you can plan to use, with the knowledge of your cohort and the individuals within this. There'll be activities you've done many times and perhaps not considered in terms of the hidden learning opportunities that we need to grasp if we want to support children to improve in the way they make behaviour choices. I hope that works for everyone, and I apologize if it doesn't!

Activities and opportunities involving fire and fire lighting

For most forest schools, fire is an integral part of what goes on. The fire circle is an important and valued central gathering point, so much so that I even know of schools which do not allow fires but still have the fire circle in place. Children tend to have a fascination with fire and my own opinion is that we need to nurture this so that children see it for its positive contributions, rather than destructive ones. Fire warms our bodies, lights up the dark winter forest school days, dries our wet clothes. It can cook our food, make water safe through boiling, create resources for us if carefully managed (charcoal would be a simple example). Children learn to respect the fire area, with well-embedded routines, demonstrating their respect for the fire in the way they approach it and how they behave around it. They almost always love the magic of lighting a fire themselves too, and I often feel that when they do this, they are connecting in some way with our ancestors, and the joy (perhaps relief) they might have felt at nurturing an ember and creating flames.

The joy perhaps, at least for us, as our lives don't depend on our ability to harness fire, may lie in the fact that it's not easy! I've seen children struggle to light a cotton pad with a spark from a ferrocerium rod. It does take some perseverance. Children need to understand from the start that they may fail, and that for many, without the acceptance of this fact, success is impossible too. So don't just let them have a go, seize the opportunity. I like to have the conversation I mentioned earlier; to state that nine out of ten points, if they were being awarded, would be for effort, and that last point, only, would be for achieving flame. I also like to have those who have been successful (i.e., tried hard but not necessarily created a flame) coach those who have not managed yet. How good is that for their self-esteem? For children who can't accept direct praise, what a wonderful way to recognize their skills and attributes.

Cotton pads and birch bark will ignite and create flames just from a spark. Charcloth, on the other hand, will create a glowing ember but not usually flames. For that, more input is needed; we need to process the ember a little more. Usually this will involve placing the ember in a 'nest' of dry grass or something similarly fibrous. We will then blow into the nest, adding sufficient oxygen to the heat and fuel so that flames will ignite. Achieving this is a massive boost to a child's self-esteem. I've had five-year-olds manage this. If you do decide to give this a try, you can collect dry grass and store it until needed, much as our ancestors probably did, or you can buy it ready to go from supermarkets and pet shops, where it is sold as rabbit bedding. You need to ensure that you position the children so that the wind is blowing from behind them, therefore blowing smoke and sparks away from them. You might decide that you hold the nest, and they approach from behind you and blow over your shoulder. I like to place lots of the straw in a line on the woodland floor, perpendicular to the wind, and the children ignite their various bits of charcloth with a firesteel, which I can then drop into the straw at various places and cover with more straw. The children can then all crouch low to the ground, and blow collectively into the pile. It's a real team effort, and everybody succeeds in making a flame regardless of whose charcloth actually ignites first. It's very easy to manage this, even with quite a few children involved. With additional adult support, we've had a pile of straw over three metres long blown to flame! This gives you great opportunities to give children differing roles, nurture the shy, encourage the natural leaders, harness the impulsive, engage the disaffected.

Using a Kelly kettle is another opportunity to help challenging children to test and develop their resilience, determination and perseverance and, when they succeed, boost their confidence. We run the Kelly Kettle Challenge, and this can be adapted for different children. For those who need the boost the most, we might even provide everything they need: kindling, tinder, small dry sticks and so on. The challenge is that they boil some water and make a brew, perhaps for themselves, perhaps for the leaders or even their parents who are due to arrive. Imagine the boost to their esteem and sense of self-sufficiency; this is a great exercise for children lacking resilience. Once they've been successful at this, we offer them the chance to prepare a meal for the group, cooking it in a hangi, or ground oven. It's something that looks impressive when the hangi is uncovered, steam billowing out and cooked food being revealed!

The Group Bow Drill Challenge is another wonderful activity. It can arise through children asking about primitive fire lighting (it has for me many times), or it could be something we plan to do, to help the group to form in a positive and effective way. I might use it in this way if we are working with a group who perhaps are newly formed, don't really know each other yet and are trying to settle as a group. Those of you who know how to use the bow drill to create fire will just need to increase the size of the bow drill set so that it can be operated by many as opposed to one person, which is what you're probably used to. It certainly does help if you can create fire this way yourself, and is a great way of firing enthusiasm, if you can demonstrate it first. But in truth, you don't need to be able to. I've never had a group who can't at least create smoke, so I always tell them, that would be the furthest I could expect them to get with the technique.

If you're unsure how this would work then, you will need a small number of resources. As always, water to extinguish the flames and a first aid kit – these should go without saying, although now I've said them. Then you will need a bow (sometimes, or just a length of rope), a drill, a hearth, a bearing block, an ember pan and a few tools. If you use a bow, it will need to be of a slightly flexible greenwood, as thick as your thumb at least, and green, i.e. freshly cut and not brittle. You'll attach some cord to this; paracord is good but starter cord (for petrol lawnmowers and chainsaws) is better because it resists abrasion and will last longer. The bow should be as long as you need for your group; perhaps three children will be on either end of it (or you could have several sets of this kit, of course). I tend not to use the bow, but instead the children use a piece of static rope, like old abseil rope, simply pulling it back and forth (gloves are vital). The drill is about 45–60cm long, dead wood that has not gone soft and 'punky', with the top sharpened to a point and the base carved to a flattish surface with chamfered edges. Hazel is good, lime too. I usually make the hearth out of the same wood if I can and you will need to have bedded the drill in already, and where it has burned a circle into the hearth, cut a V-notch into this, to just short of the centre and about a sixth of the circle you have burned in. The hearth should be about 2cm thick, split deadwood, almost like a plank. The bearing block is of a green hard wood (I often cut a piece of holly for this purpose) with a tapered notch into which the 'pointy' end of the drill can sit. Make it long enough for at least two children to hold it in place. The ember pan is just a piece of bark, a flat seashell, or a wood shaving, whatever, and sits beneath the V-notch, ready to catch the ember your group will create.

That all might sound confusing, especially if the bow drill is new to you! Picture this, which will help! In the centre you have a hearth, with a V cut out of it, and the drill is sitting in the bowl shape you have already burnt into it, above the notch. An ember pan sits beneath the notch. Two or four children are standing with the bearing block, and the other end of the drill (with the point) is sitting in the small notch you have cut into it. They will press down to keep it in place, not too hard, and concentrate on keeping the drill straight and vertical. Then the bow, or rope, is wrapped once or twice around the shaft of the drill, and held by the rest of the team. They will then pull back and forth, slowly at first, but getting faster, and as the drill warms it will begin to produce smoke and embers which will gather in the V. Now, to see this smoke is a magnificent effort! If the children create a smoking ember that is self-sustaining when the drilling stops and the hearth is removed, that is magical indeed. This ember should be nurtured for a few minutes, lightly blown if needed, then transferred into a tinder bundle as above, and blown into flame. Even the most stubborn of children, who have a default comment of 'This is boring' will delight in seeing what they've created. Those who chose not to take part will be drawn in. You'll have developed the skills of teamwork, co-ordinated effort, encouragement, communication, trust, leadership...the list goes on. If you're still unsure, a YouTube search for 'team bow drill' will show you how it looks. I've done this with adults, college students and primary groups. It is brilliant and well worth a go.

General fire lighting can present yet more valuable learning moments. For example, think of some children you work with who have some or all of these issues: perhaps they struggle to follow instructions, they might not think before they act, they don't get the idea of logical processes – one thing naturally follows another, cause and effect and so on. Does that sound like some children you know? Let them have a go at fire lighting but remember to tell them, 'Preparation means success. If you fail to prepare, you prepare to fail.' They need to gather two big bundles of matchstick dry (and matchstick thin) twigs, as long as their forearm. They need to clear the ground down to bare soil, place a few split logs down as a base, have a tinder bundle ready, gather some thin fuel and some larger fuel. Then give them the firesteel, matches, lighter, whatever you are using, and the tinder (cotton pads, paper or birch bark). Some children will not gather enough kindling, which will mean the fire won't last. Others will not gather enough thin fuel, and as a result, the tinder and kindling will burn away before it has ignited the next level of fuel. Failure? No. Learning opportunity? Yes. This is a great activity for children to begin to learn about cause and effect, and thinking ahead so they can plan efficiently. It also means that children get the opportunity to see that a lack of success does not have to be anything other than the first step to getting fire. Clearly, children who exhibit low resilience can learn here to increase that resilience over time. They also learn to cope with the prospect of 'failure' if they continue to see it as such, but even better if they can change their perspective and allow failure just to be part of a process and nothing to be scared of.

Opportunities and activities involving den building

Most forest schools' programmes will at some point have den building going on; we have children who love to build them on a small scale, for little action figures which we have in a box, ready to go. Some will decide they want to build a 'base' of some sort, others get really interested in how our ancestors lived, and yet others will want a large communal den of more elaborate construction. We currently have two Mesolithic 'hunter-gatherer' shelters on one of our sites.

These are great for presenting us with more opportunities to develop team skills. Children who don't think they can 'do it' can start small and build from there. Children who lack empathy need us only to initiate a discussion along the lines of, 'What would it be like if this shelter was your home for a whole year?'

I enjoy the larger builds involving several children because it gives everyone a chance to shine and to be appreciated for what they bring to the task. Some, for example, might not be physically able to contribute so much, but will stand back and offer ideas. Often the child who does this sees the whole picture rather than being focused on one element of the build to the exclusion of the rest. From this perspective, they can pre-empt problems. The wise facilitator can use this during a review to encourage participants to value the different skills and qualities the group bring to the build, and this is wonderful for group cohesion. It is also a wonderful opportunity for the children to sit in such a big shelter together and feel that sense of empathy, belonging and community, where perhaps that previously did not exist.

Some of our children recently became interested in a wren's nest they had discovered, which naturally led to wondering how a wren, or indeed other nesting birds, actually begins a nest. Before long the children were trying to build their own nest in a low shrub. Others had stuck half a dozen sycamore stems in the ground and were busy trying to weave a nest around these. It was a wonderful opportunity for a connection with nature but also to develop their empathy; they discussed how it might feel for a bird to be sitting in the woods during stormy weather and driving rain. They then applied this same thought process to our resident roe deer, and even homeless people. In a world where empathy does seem increasingly to be lacking, it was pleasing to see. A different kind of shelter building to be sure, but valuable outcomes all the same.

Tarps and hammocks offer further opportunities. These are a more complex type of shelter, which requires an understanding of useful knots in order to put up a hammock safely, protected properly by a tarp over the top, pegged out so that it will shed any rain. I like to use this exercise to improve relationships; this might be my own with the harder to reach young people I work with, or relationships within the group. I do this by picking out a couple of learners who have grasped the knot tying quickly. All the better if these children are new to the group, less 'popular' or perhaps children I am personally struggling with in terms of building an effective working relationship. I'll then promote these children as 'knot wizards' or whatever moniker works, and ask or allow them to support the others. Kids who can't cope with praise will like this, as will those with lower status in the group. This is called status boosting and I've seen it used very effectively. I had a colleague called Dan who would use this with vulnerable young students each year, boosting their own esteem at the same time as presenting them as high status within their peer group.

One of the fundamental elements of shelter building that I feel is beneficial for children who need to develop their ability to make better behaviour choices is the need to manage risk. It is often the case that children who have complex issues, and certain diagnoses such as types of attention deficit, will be risk takers. There's nothing inherently wrong with this, of course, and in many ways, settings and situations it can be a prized quality. However, with some children it is coupled with an inability to mitigate for, or even recognize, danger and risk. Whether you are putting up a hammock which someone must lie in, or building a roofed shelter that your classmates are going to get under, risk is there. Even in the siting of your tarp or shelter, you teach the children to assess risk; look up for deadwood that could ruin your day, look down for signs of animal trails, water flow, ant trails. Any trip hazards? As a leader, you need to be active in the process of planning the build. This is where we find other ways to say 'be careful'. If I find myself about to say, 'Be careful you don't...' or, 'Be careful how you...', then I quickly rephrase: 'How might you keep yourself safe with all these wet roots around?' or, in the case of a hammock, 'How might you tie that so it will take your weight?' With a group shelter, I'm asking questions like, 'How much weight do you think that roof can hold? How could you make it stronger?'

When you are aware of needs and ask these questions, you're making changes to the way a child thinks about risk. I think this is vital work when your clients do not have the habit of understanding risk. This is a truly transferable skill: what they learn in the woods with you, they will use in other elements of their life, as you are supporting them to learn a process, rather than a specific skill. Additionally, learning to build a shelter using only what the woods provide can make a child feel a real sense of self-reliance and confidence that can be lacking. And remember, much of the poor behaviour we see is driven by anxiety, low resilience and low confidence, so by addressing these we are beginning to support the child to make changes to their behaviour choices.

Activities and opportunities involving natural crafts

There is something inherent in honest physical work that appeals to many adults. We sometimes run courses for grown-ups as well as children, and watching the satisfaction a 40-something adult displays having carved a spoon, or made a bark container or longbow, is ample proof that there is something in us all that benefits from working with our hands. The 'rustic' look of natural products such as bramble baskets means that, although five children might produce five very different looking containers, they're all 'right'! Comparisons might occur, but no judgements are made. Children are often naturally drawn towards 'making stuff' at our forest schools, as a natural follow-up to exploring the nature of materials in the woods, be they nettle fibres, flexible bark or mud! All we need to do is recognize and harness the opportunities that gives us to support children with their behaviour. What is marvellous about this is that it takes little effort! Both children and adults can get themselves in a meditative state when working on crafts and using natural materials.

Years ago, I worked at a school where we ran a residential week in the Borrowdale Valley in the English Lake District. For years, we would run a non-stop programme of activities; our teenage students were SEMH, inner-city kids. These children were never left with their engines idling because that could lead to them finding their own entertainment, which was often not positive. So, through our meticulously planned week, they'd be up a mountain in the morning, ghyll scrambling in the afternoon, canoeing in the evening. In truth, these were brilliant weeks, exhausting but fun. We almost always got great behaviour and children finished the week as different people from when they started. It was that good, because our team was that good. Then we introduced bushcraft and forest school to the school and we decided that we wanted our kids to learn how to be relaxed – busy doing nothing, so to speak. This was a big ask, given diagnoses, including ADHD, CD and ODD, to name a few. We had seen some positives come the previous year with crafts, and so we introduced whittling, carving and archery to our days in the Lakes. The effect was amazing. Our learners would sit in their camp chairs, chatting, carving spoons and getting on – just sharing information with each other, talking about family issues, sharing feelings. There were truly 'goosebumpy' moments for us as staff. All we'd needed to do was offer the opportunity. Our great residentials became even better. The point of this little anecdote is that it doesn't need lots of additional effort to introduce a very positive experience to your most challenging children.

Spoon or utensil carving is a great activity, and with the right wood selected, is accessible for younger children. I might have a mixed-age group, with the older children carving spoons and using crook knives, while the younger ones can carve a simple spreading knife or spatula. I tend to pick a type of wood that's easier to carve; not holly or elm, for example, but perhaps young green ash, hazel or sycamore, although sycamore can be very slippery once you remove the bark. I won't go into knife safety and glove use here, of course; you will have done that on your training, or if you've yet to qualify as a forest school leader, it will be included in your training. The planning itself is great in that it requires a child to think ahead, anticipate problems and plan to avoid them or deal with them. You can see that such skills will be hugely beneficial for children with behaviour issues, who often don't consider problems until after they've occurred. We want to introduce them to a new way of thinking here. So as facilitators, we've got a little more to do than 'Here's how you carve a knife/spoon.'

I like to facilitate this thinking process: 'Do you think the bowl of the spoon will be easy to hold on to while you're carving? If not, what can we do to make it easier?' I should say here that I like to leave a 'handle' protruding from the end of the spoon bowl, to hold on to when I'm carving. Usually the last thing I do is to remove this and tidy up the spoon. Children will also note that the grain is harder to work in one direction than another. This can require them to cut towards themselves, and again, this can be done safely with planning. For those who don't know, we use a reinforced grip with one hand holding the knife, and the fingers of both hands on the back of the blade, pushing it (importantly, you must not pull with your knife hand, just push with your fingers). That way, it is impossible to cut yourself, because your fingers are not long enough to push the blade far enough to hit you. This is risk management for children who haven't learned how to risk manage, it's danger awareness for risk takers, it's self-regulation for those who struggle to self-regulate, and it introduces focus to those who are inattentive. Add to that relaxation, a meditative state, time to talk and a sense of accomplishment, and you have a simple activity that is great for most of our learners, and priceless for our complex children.

Making natural cordage is another activity that presents opportunities for children to relax in that strangely meditative state of soft fascination where they are focused on a task to the exclusion of all else. I like to take them through the process in stages. This is a great model to use for the inattentive, breaking the task up into smaller, more achievable tasks. It also reduces the risk of overwhelming those who have low resilience or might be demand avoidant. Our first task might be the safe harvesting of materials. The children need to be able to identify the resource (nettles, brambles, willowherb, certain inner barks, perhaps). This presents more opportunities to think ahead: where will we find these, how do we gather them safely, do we need gloves, how many stems do we need? Once gathered, we need to process the materials, so with nettles, for example, that requires us to separate the outer stalk fibres from the inner ones, and keep the inner parts. Then we may decide to dry them, or just use them as they are. We will separate them to get the thickness we need. The next part of the process is to twist them together to create cordage, knowing when and how to add new fibres.

As well as the process of thinking ahead, and the relaxation it offers, cordage making is a great activity because we can point out to the children that we can create something immensely strong and useful, if we are happy to put in the work, through several stages. When a child is struggling through a behaviour incident, and perhaps I am using that ABC conversation we mentioned earlier, then I could remind them of the cordage making. I want them to see that, in the same way that they can produce a useful resource through breaking a task down into small parts and working through a process, so they can change the way they behave using the same model. So here we find another transferrable process, from practical tasks to self-management. Remember, the model of behaviour management here is not that you control others, it's that you support them to learn to control themselves.

Other opportunities and activities

I should imagine by now that you are thinking about the frequently occurring activities in your forest school and how you can seize learning opportunities that abound in these situations. The truth is that we can often find missed learning moments in most of the common tasks. It is really just a case of looking at them with new eyes and a heightened level of awareness. So let's look at a small number of other common woodland activities, planned or otherwise, and draw conclusions about what benefits they might offer, should we decide to highlight them to children.

At one of our sites, we are working with a learner currently who has low self-esteem, lacks confidence and resilience and can find social situations somewhat awkward. We have given this learner a role in greeting all new children, showing them around the site and introducing them to other children. Effectively, the newcomer is taken under the wing of this person. We have conveyed our absolute belief in our 'meeter and greeter' that the job will be done well, does not require any supervision on our part and that trust is absolute. This young person has not experienced much like this before and has risen to the role. We would recommend that you consider taking this sort of 'risk' with similar learners. I equate it sometimes to giving David Beckham the captaincy of England, but let's not go into that... Suffice to say that if we demonstrate our belief and confidence in this way, children will usually rise to it. This presents you with moments to give praise, which the child will value. Your relationship with that child will be consolidated, and be there to fall back on when that child is not doing so well with behaviour choices. If the child you are considering trying this on (and I hope you are) sometimes seeks attention through poor, odd or even bizarre behaviour, you can now show them that there are better ways to get attention. You can also lavish unsolicited attention on them at times. So, consider having mentor roles if your forest school set-up allows this.

Journey sticks might be familiar to you as these are a well-used activity in many forest schools. For those who don't know, they are essentially sticks onto which, using string or wool, you will attach items that in some way represent your journey through the woods. The children in our woods prepare their sticks, then we encourage them to wander a route, collecting items. These might be plants they notice, curious sticks, pine cones or other fruits, seed heads, leaves, whatever they find. Feathers, bones, empty chrysalis remains and man-made items can be included, and children will often find many more curious items! I like to get children to then guide another child through their journey, using the items on the journey stick. This is great as a way to gently introduce interaction with others, to those who perhaps for various reasons struggle with their social skills. We don't force anyone, of course, and some children are more comfortable with leading an adult round, but it is a useful means of extending the usual journey stick activity in a way that helps with social interaction. With some groups, we've even used the journey sticks as a representation of their journey through life, and this can be a fascinating exercise for those who have had adverse childhood experiences. This approach should be used with caution and perhaps with guidance from other professionals, of course. I recently designed a programme for military veterans with PTSD where I built this activity in for them also.

Seasonal activities can also offer great opportunities which can be used to support behaviour change. On forest school sessions in our organization, we love the John Muir Award for this reason. While children are learning over an extended period about their environment, they are also developing understanding and empathy for it, a sense of belonging and stewardship, and a confidence in sharing that knowledge with others. We like children to experience the woodland in all seasons, and, of course, forest school should be a long-term intervention, so the award fits nicely into this. I would encourage all forest school leaders to look into the John Muir Award. The four 'challenges' of the award are discover, explore, conserve and share. The wild place they use can be as small as a back garden or school grounds, so a woodland is brilliant. These challenges create a wonderful framework onto which you can hang your activities that address social and emotional issues. For example, during the conserve challenge, the children must take personal responsibility for the wild place. This is wonderful for children who struggle to take responsibility for their behaviour (when it is appropriate) or who always present that external locus of control that suggests it's 'never my fault'. I particularly love the share element of the John Muir Award. Our learners will usually plan a celebratory event, invite parents or carers, cater for them, present their wild place and their new-found knowledge. You will see relationships blossom, communication skills develop, craft skills improve, and their pride in themselves will increase enormously. They might want to build a stage for presentations, or make seats for their parents, put up tarps for cover from the weather, take differing roles in the whole process; it's wonderful. I'd recommend that you check out the award online and go for it!

Other seasonal activities might include types of shelter building specific to the season, including leaf litter shelters in autumn, and snow shelters in winter. I show the children how to build either a quinze with powder snow, or an igloo, using snow compressed into a plastic box to make bricks. These activities require lots of collaboration, discussion and teamwork and are great for all children, but perhaps those who benefit most comprehensively are those who already have a deficit of such skills. Organizing an event for their parents for Halloween, Beltane and Samhain offers more opportunities for our learners to develop team skills, confidence and a sense of accomplishment that boosts their self-esteem. Children will also love elf carving at Christmas time (some of our children would and do carve them all year round!) and this is another activity that requires little in the way of preparation, but offers a chance for children to hone their skills of risk management, perseverance and independence, focus and patience. We probably all know children, and some adults, come to think of it, who would benefit from that! The children basically carve a stick (about 2.5cm diameter) to a blunt point, which will be the top of the elf's hat. They then carve a little mouth, add some details with felt tips or paints, glue on a bobble at the top of the hat, made from cotton wool, perhaps add a beard, and get as creative as they like! Older children will enjoy making these for younger siblings or cousins. We've found that children of all ages love making them!

Chapter 9

TEAM-BUILDING GAMES: ADD-ONS TO YOUR FOREST SCHOOL

Although team-building and problem-solving games do not seem to fit with the forest school 'way', and are generally seen as sitting perhaps more comfortably with 'traditional' outdoor education, we do include such activities when we are working with complex cases. The reason for this is that they work, and it feels remiss of us not to use these activities to support children. Equally, they don't need to be mammoth tasks; raft building might be beyond your scope, for example, but that doesn't mean you can't introduce problem solving to your repertoire. For two decades, I delivered a personal, social, health and economic (PSHE) curriculum to secondary-age learners with what was then labelled social, emotional and behavioural difficulties. They'd do many of the activities I discuss below, and I can barely remember any cases where they tried to opt out. Most valuable in this entire process was the whole review model used after activities, some examples of which I will include here.

My tendency with problem solving and team building in general forest school days is to have some on standby to use, rather than plan for them, as I might do for example if I'm running a course specifically for a complex needs group. But once you've introduced a forest school group to one or two of these activities, perhaps when they have a spare ten minutes before the end of a day, you need to expect that the children will ask to do more, as they are often well received! If I see an issue with a group that needs to be resolved – maybe there is a lack of trust within the group, or the lack of group cohesion is obstructive – then I might deliberately build in these activities.

I do like the bigger tasks, what we would have called command tasks when I was in the military. Raft building is an example, bridge building might be another. These can be scaled down, of course. A great challenge to the group's skills is to ask them to use their knot knowledge, tool skills and understanding of natural materials to build a small bridge, perhaps across a small gap or from tree stump to tree stump, which will bear the weight of a remote-controlled car driven across it. You can limit tools and materials if you wish. I usually allow them a number of saplings, some string, a knife, maybe some bark strips. Groups of about six children are best. As with all the activities mentioned here, children will take various roles. You as facilitator may influence this, in your efforts to milk the activity for all it's worth, perhaps choosing certain learners for roles based on the skills you'd like them to develop.

Another activity I like is called Nuclear Rod. I cordon off an area with mine tape, maybe about three or four metres square (usually a tree at each corner can dictate the size). In the centre of the area I place a straight hazel rod, and I then drop a tube of some description (I use a container from a well-known brand of crisps) down the stick. The group are told this is a nuclear rod which must be removed in a set time, in order to reduce the heat of the core and avoid a catastrophe...you get the picture! Obviously, the children cannot enter the area, or even hang over it, but they have two ropes. That's it! You can add further restrictions if you like, or try different resources, maybe sticky tape, natural cordage, whatever. A similar activity is to place a ping-pong ball in a bowl in the centre, and the group get a plastic jug (with a handle is best), two lengths of paracord, long enough to reach from one side of the area to another, and crucially, access to a water supply. They must remove the ball. Perhaps dropping in the fact that a ping-pong ball floats might be helpful for some groups...

With tasks like these, you observe carefully, perhaps offer small amounts of advice, and notice which roles are taken by which learners, who is being listened to and who is not, even though they have great ideas. Then you look to review. I use the plan-perform-evaluate method and the review phase fits into this evaluation. Reviewing can consist of facilitating discussion with well-thought-out questions. I like to keep children moving during reviews, so I might get them to stand in a line in front of me, and ask them to take one, two or three steps forward if they agree with a statement I make, or the same backwards, depending on how much they might disagree. I might ask them to close their eyes when they step, if I'm concerned they will be influenced by others. Questions or statements might include 'The group worked well as a team'; 'I felt as if my contribution was valued'; 'I think we could do that better'. Then, comparing where each person is standing, how many steps they took and in what direction, provides an interesting stimulus for discussion. You could have a continuum marked out on the floor, from one to ten, where one is 'totally disagree' and ten is 'totally agree'. You could get children to do a 'thumbs-up, thumbs-down, intermediate' as a way of measuring too. How you choose to do that is not as important as the discussion it generates.

I like to do activities that develop and build trust and these might include blindfold guiding in the woods, perhaps where one child guides another blindfolded child by their hand to a certain tree, then moves them away, removes the blindfold and the child must find the tree by feel. This is a great sensory experience, but also develops trust. Taking it further, a blindfolded child can be guided round an obstacle course from a start point to a finish, with verbal communication only.

Trust falls and trust dives are also brilliant activities. They do need to be well managed but have terrific value. I might therefore start these activities with something like the Back to Back Sit Challenge, where learners need to stand back to back and then sit down, supporting each other as they go. This can progress to facing each other and linking hands (Counterbalance Sit) and then perhaps the Circle Sit Challenge. During this activity, the entire group (or perhaps split into two groups) will stand in a circle and shuffle until they are tight together, all with their left shoulders facing into the centre, so that they are chest to back, tight together. Then, in a co-ordinated way, they all sit on the knee of the person behind! If they trust each other and go for it, it is possible for the whole group to be sitting down in a big, self-supporting circle! If one person falters... It's best to play this on a grassy field!

Other trust games include Human Knot. All the group stand bunched together, with their right hands in the air, and grab another hand. They then place their left hands in the air, and grab a random left hand. Next, they pull slowly apart, keeping hold of those hands. Now, without letting go, they have to unravel the resultant knot. It's a nice activity and a good game after the group have got to know each other a little. There are lots of ice breakers you can try to speed up the process of getting to know each other. Here are a few.

Skin the Snake requires the group to stand in a queue. They all raise their right hands and place their left hands through their own legs and behind them. They each grab the protruding hand of the person in front of them with their right hand and then the person at the end of the line crawls through the legs of the person in front, without letting go; that person follows them through the third person's legs, who follows on, and on, and on, until you skin the snake. Ice well and truly broken! If that's a little risky, play Greetings of the World. Get the group in a circle and explain to them that they are going to use different ways of greeting each other, from different cultures and countries around the world. That could include bowing formally to each other, shaking hands, high fives, big Russian bear hugs, kissing both cheeks *à la France*, and so on.

Problem-solving activities have great value for all children and I especially like to use them with children who have complex and special needs, including those who exhibit behaviour issues. The reason for this is that they have at their heart a positivity about problems – here we have an obstacle, how do we plan to overcome it? I think that is a mentality we need to nurture in our young people. As well as the tasks mentioned earlier, here are a couple that need less equipment.

For Circle the Circle, in schools, I use two different sized hula hoops. In the woods, I like to fashion hoops out of willow, of about the same size as hula hoops (but again, one smaller than the other). The group stand in a circle, linking hands, and I place one hoop somewhere in the circle, by getting two of the participants to unlink and then grasp hands through the hoop. This hoop must then travel all the way round the circle, without anyone letting go of hands, and get back to the start. This necessitates children stepping through the hoop as it arrives, perhaps flicking it from shoulder to shoulder as they go, although there are other ways... Once they've done that, evaluate it and see how they could improve their performance and speed things up. Then try again. I then add the other hoop at a different point in the circle and one goes clockwise, one anti-clockwise, hence the need for the hoops to be of different sizes as they're going to meet at some point. This is great fun, with real learning taking place.

Speed Ball works similarly in the plan-perform-evaluate model. With the children standing in a circle (ten people is a good minimum), give them a beach ball, and explain it needs to travel all the way round the circle as fast as they can, missing nobody. Time them and aim to be faster each time. They'll get it down to under ten seconds before you tell them that the record is less than a second... Plan again...

Communication games are great for all kids too. Sometimes communication is as much about listening as it is about speaking, and many children struggle to give listening the attention that is expected. ADHD children will benefit from learning a little more focus in this way and so too will many other SEND children. I always explain to children that when a communication task is not as successful as we might want, it is not somebody's fault, it is more likely a breakdown in communication. You might have said exactly what you wanted from your partner, they might have done exactly as they heard you ask them, but that does not mean you succeed. See below.

Back to Back Sticks is a great activity. Prepare two sets of identical materials. In the woods, that might be six hazel sticks per child; maybe two at 4cm, two at 8cm and two at 12cm. Add to this two broadly similar holly leaves, two matching pine cones, maybe bones, feathers, and so on but all roughly the same. The children then sit back to back on the woodland floor. Child A places the items down in front of them one at a time, explaining their position, angle, direction to Child B, who copies with their items. This continues until Child A has placed every item and explained this to Child B, who has done likewise. They then compare their compositions and see how different they are. From this they can talk about where the communication broke down and how to improve it. You might decide only Child A can talk, or introduce that restriction as they improve. If both can talk then there's a valuable lesson to learn in feeding back to ensure you understand; something that catches certain kids out all of the time and results in them getting into trouble in class, for example. A back to back drawing activity, perhaps with charcoal they have made on the fire themselves, is equally good.

If you want to help children develop their listening skills, or at least get them to recognize how important listening is, then there are a few activities you can set up quickly. Black Magic is one I use a lot, and I need an accomplice, so I usually choose an oppositional or defiant child with whom I haven't quite got a relationship yet (killing two birds with one stone). I tell the children that I am a mind reader. I will step away, and they choose an item in the woods (this could be as small as a beech nut, or as big as a beech tree). They share that information with my 'assistant'. I then return and the assistant asks me a series of 'Is it the...?' questions. Lo and behold, when the assistant gets to their item, I say yes! Do this a few times and the children will be baffled. Explain to them that they need to focus and see if they can pick up on the communication that they're missing. In fact, it could be that you've agreed with your assistant that the sixth item they ask about is the right one, or they will scratch their nose as they ask about the chosen item, but I usually ask them to add a colour to the item before the object the group chose. So: 'Is it the tree?' No. 'Is it Paul's boots?' No. 'Is it the firesteel?' No. 'Is it the GREEN rucksack?' No. 'Is it the pine cone?' Yes! This might require a lot of focus from the group, and particularly from individuals who need to develop that skill, which is what we want, of course.

Giving a group of blindfolded children a length of rope and asking them, as a team, to lay it out in an exact square is another good communication game, as is having one child direct the rest to put up a simple tent blindfolded (I use an old-fashioned Force Ten tent for this). Swampstompers is another. First you need to make your swampstompers; these are scaffold planks, with holes drilled in them every metre and close to each end. Tie old rope through these, one end knotted beneath and about a metre length protruding out of the top of the board. Children stand on the two stompers like skis, as many as you have space for. They need to co-ordinate and communicate really well to then walk around on the stompers. I usually say these will help them walk out of a swamp safely, hence the name.

There are many more games and variations on these that will help you to develop these vital skills with your learners. A quick search on the internet will help and there are lots of good books on the subject too – so start searching!

Chapter 10

CONCLUSION

I do hope this book has been an interesting and informative read for you. I hope also that you can see where there is a need to fit this model in to forest school, even where it moves away from the child-led philosophy we all love. I passionately believe that forest school is incredibly important; that, in fact, forest school, devoid of outcomes and measurable results, should be the right of every child in our education system (and those home-educated children too). In writing this book, I seek only to give some tips for how we can support all children to access what is an immensely valuable experience.

Within these pages, we've looked at specific needs and strategies we can use to support those needs. Remember that a child may not have a diagnosed condition but may display many of the traits we've looked at. In that case, don't be scared to apply some of the techniques and see what the impact is. Additionally, remember that no child is just the label, and the better you know a youngster, the more effective your ability to select an appropriate tool. I hope that you adopt the healthy curiosity that I talked about early in the book

– that positivity and determination to understand the behaviour in front of you and see its function and context. Once you've cracked that, the rest is (a little) easier!

We've discussed how important your perspective is. In many schools and provisions, you can see staff who are confrontational, punitive and bullying in their approach. You might know some yourself; they are in primary, secondary and special schools everywhere, in my experience. Some of them are stuck in their ways, others too lazy to change, and others just don't know what else they could do. Try not to be too judgemental about this; we are all at different points in the journey and we can all improve. I am certainly someone who has moved on from being a shouter and a confronter. While those things worked for me (and do for others) in a very superficial way, they don't do anything to improve the likelihood of you enjoying your job. Staying on that path is what leads you to be the tainted old cynic sitting in the corner of the staffroom, insisting, 'I've seen all of this before...' I'd advise you to have faith in a positive perspective, a lively curiosity and a belief that we get more of the kind of behaviour that we pay the most attention to. Notice what children do right, pounce on it if it's rare, and things will improve. Apply sanctions when they're required, and apply them with regret. Let the child know you believe they can do better. I believe they eventually will, if you do that.

We've covered how you can manage the general school population and their behaviour too; this is important because if we only apply oil to the squeakiest wheel, it won't be long before the other wheels start to squeak for attention too! That is where your routines, expectations and ethos will make all the difference, of course. Make it easy for children to make good behaviour choices and the vast majority will do just that. Make it difficult for them to make bad choices, and this will 'mop up' a few more. Then you can apply the more advanced techniques we explored for the remainder. That's how the best behaviour managers work, and that's how the best teachers work with diverse groups of children in one group, without too much difficulty. In my role as a behaviour consultant I always say to colleagues during training events that anyone can manage the most challenging children; it's just a case of going from 'I don't know how' to 'I do know how'. It's the essence of teaching, really. Now, if you started this book thinking, 'These kids are a nightmare in forest school...I don't know how to deal with them', I hope you now feel better equipped to do so. If not, then get in touch with me! What I will give you here is a cast-iron guarantee, which I share with all colleagues I meet. If you email me with a behaviour problem, I'll get back to you with a solution. It might take a while; I might need to consult with colleagues. But I'll get back to you, and like all good teachers and all good forest school leaders, I'll seem as if I've known forever that which I only learned the night before!

Dave
Consulo Education
Out There Adventures

ACKNOWLEDGEMENTS

I owe thanks to far too many people, for far too many reasons, to name them all there. I hope my gratitude has always been clear to them. I learned my craft as a behaviour support at the knees of a number of wonderful practitioners, and so it's easiest to thank the entity that was Springwell Dene School in Sunderland, rather than individual staff. It was, as I once said to an Ofsted inspector (I was a teaching assistant at the time), 'a little piece of magic'.

Pauline Holbrook has said to me on many occasions, 'Why don't you write a book?' The first time I sat down to do this, it turned into my behaviour management app, Behaviour Ninja. This time, it's a book. Thanks, Pauline!

I learned the magic of forest schools through a course run by Richard Wood. He has offered me advice during the writing of this book and every word he speaks is gold; he truly knows forest school and I'm grateful to him for his help. Barry Simpson and John Coates are the colleagues I currently work with. To watch them daily, managing challenging young people and allowing those children to flourish, is a treat. We have children who require one-to-one support in other settings, yet present no issues at our various woods and this is because of the talents of these guys.

At JKP, Emily Badger, Development Editor, has been patient with me when I've struggled to hit (or more accurately missed) deadlines. Her advice is honest, specific and straightforward, which is the only way it can work for me. Cheers, Emily!

Thanks to my family for their patience. Bank holiday weekends, spent in the house so I can work; piles of notes and scribbles everywhere and just sitting with me as I reach a deadline – all of this has been much appreciated. Thanks especially to Jen, my wonderful wife.

Finally, thanks to the Out There Clan, our woodland wonders, the kids who attend our forest schools, who participate in our specialist courses and who make the job fun! To them and all the young people who have helped me to learn, many thanks. Keep doing what you're doing!

FURTHER READING

Books

MacDonald, S. (2016). *The Little Book of Team Games*. London: Bloomsbury.

Rohnke, K. (1984). *Silver Bullets: A Guide to Initiative Problems, Adventure Games and Trust Activities*. Dubuque, IA: Kendall/Hunt Publishing.

Rohnke, K. (1989). *Cowstails and Cobras II: A Guide to Games, Initiatives, Ropes Courses and Adventure Curriculum*. Dubuque, IA: Kendall/Hunt Publishing.

Sonnet, H. & Barnes, R. (2003). *101 Games for Social Skills*. Hyde: LDA Publishing.

Websites

https://thequeenmomma.com/team-building-activities-for-kids

www.twinkl.co.uk/blog/fun-team-building-activities-for-kids

INDEX